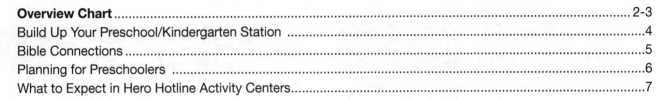

Congratulations!

Preschool/Kindergarten Leader

T0022519

Hero Hotline:
Called Together to Serve God!

	Bible Story	Hotline Tips	Music	Crafts
Session 1	Jesus Builds the Team John 1:35-51	Heroes are called to… Follow Jesus!	• Hero Hotline Theme Song • If U Wanna Be A Hero	• Hotline Comics • Hotline Cuff
Session 2	Shiphrah, Puah, and Miriam: God's Wonder Women Exodus 1:8–2:10	Heroes are called to… Help Others!	• Hold Up • Beat Like Yours	• Helping Hero Medal • Basket of Blessings
Session 3	Jethro Mentors Moses Exodus 18	Heroes are called to… Work Together!	• Let's Strive • Work Together	• Hero Puppet Team • Work Together Painting
Session 4	The Magnificent Magi Matthew 2:1-12	Heroes are called to… Listen to God!	• Good Good Life • Show Grace, Speak Truth	• Magi's Guiding Star • Hero Shield • Stars and Straws
Session 5	Unexpected Heroes Give Paul a Basket Ride Acts 9:1-25	Heroes are called to… Show Grace!	• Your Grace • That's What Makes A Hero	• Hero Team Frame

Hero Verse

So let's strive for the things that bring peace and the things that build each other up. (Romans 14:19)

Science	Recreation	Snacks	Notes
• Magnetic Attraction • Sinking Soda	• Hero Quick-Change • Heroic Catch • Hero Headquarters • Preschool Recreation	• Build Your Own Fig Tree • Super Vision Sticks • Nathanael's Fig Tree Fruit Bars	
• Bubbling Up • Super Straw	• Hero Helping Toss • Don't Wake the Baby • Practice Makes Heroes • Preschool Recreation	• Hope Heroes • Pretzel Power Lifts • Banana Boats	
• Power Paper • Super Bubble Blower	• Work Together Tag • Find the Team • Quickening Questions • Preschool Recreation	• Healthy Campfire • Campfire Trail Mix • Work Together Pizza	
• The Leak-Proof Bag • Looking for the Star	• Guided by a Star • Return Home Another Way • Heroic Attention • Preschool Recreation	• Colossal Courage Cookies • Veggie Treasures • Hero Ropes	
• Flying Ping-Pong Ball • Incredible Ice • Bonus Experiment: Liquid Light	• Grace Tag • Team Up! • Build a Basket • Preschool Recreation	• Marvelous Mini Cakes • Cones of Power • Basket Snacks	

Build Up Your Preschool/Kindergarten Station
Get Ready to Work Together at the Hero Hotline!

Dress the part, Preschool/Kindergarten Leader!
Have fun dressing up as Superheroes. Add hero touches like a cape and mask. Wear your Hero Hotline Leader T-Shirt and other comfortable clothing. Preschool and Kindergarten leaders often may get down on the floor with children, so it is important to dress appropriately.

Who's Who at Hero Hotline:
VBS Participants: Heroes
Rotation Guides: Sidekick
Activity Center Leaders: Station Leaders
Gathering Time Leader: Professor
Puppet: Super Meer

Choose fun group names!
Coordinate theme-related preschool group names with your VBS director. See the Director Guide for ideas!

Working Together to Bring Peace

Hero Hotline VBS is based on Romans 14:19: "So let's strive for the things that bring peace and the things that build each other up." This verse reminds us that God calls us to be a part of a community—working to bring peace to the world is something that we are all called to do together.

Here's how Hero Hotline helps Heroes work together to bring peace and build one another up:

The Hero Hotline Headquarters is a secret place where Heroes go to help solve problems called in by other heroes out in the community. At Hero Hotline, everyone's gifts are valued and each Hero has a role to play. Heroes receive a call/assignment each day by the Professor and Super Meer to help solve a problem that other Heroes in the community are facing. Heroes will then explore the files and database of the Hero Hotline to discover how Heroes can work together to bring peace.

Peace comes from God, and as God's people we are called to share that peace with the world. We work together, help one another, and encourage one another because God has called us to live in community and fellowship with one another. We all can strive, in both expected and unexpected ways, to bring peace, love, and justice to the world.

Here's how each session will highlight the ways we can work together as a team to strive for peace and build each other up:

- *By recognizing that we are all a part of the family of God by our faith in Jesus.* Just as the disciples were called to follow Jesus, we are also called to follow and be a part of his team.

- *By recognizing that our faith in God calls us to help others in need and stand up for what is right.* Just like Shiphrah, Puah, and Miriam stood up against the injustices of Pharaoh, we can speak up for those who need help.

- *By learning that Heroes can't go it alone!* Just like Moses took his father-in-law's advice to build a team of people to help share the load, we too can look to mentors and friends to work alongside us to do what God has called us to do.

- *By discovering that God speaks to and directs us in many ways*. Just like the magi were directed by a star and a dream, we can receive God's words and direction when we pay attention to the Bible, creation, the people God puts in our lives, and so many other ways.

- *By finding ways to show grace to others.* Paul's story began with grace being offered to him, both from Jesus and from some of the other disciples. People who once didn't like Paul helped him to safety! We too can offer grace to those around us.

Planning for Preschoolers & Kindergartners

Self-Contained VBS

In a self-contained VBS, preschoolers and/or kindergartners stay in one dedicated room/area for all activities. This book provides the resources and tools you need for a self-contained VBS, but you may also find helpful alternatives in the elementary-age station leader books.

Here is one possible schedule you could use:

Self-Contained PreK/K Class Schedule		
Activity	Suggested Times (in minutes)	
	Two hours	Three hours
Gathering Time with Super Meer	10	20
Bible Story	15	25
Science Time	15	25
Craft Time	20	30
Recreation Time	20	25
Snack Time/Missions	15	20
Music Time	15	20
Reflection Time	10	15

Rotation Model VBS

In a rotation model VBS, preschoolers and/or kindergartners move to different areas for each activity. Heroes may rotate to the same centers as elementary-age Heroes, with some age-appropriate adaptations that can be found in this book or other elementary-age station leader books.

Here is one possible schedule you could use:

Rotation Model PreK/K Class Schedule		
Activity	Suggested Times (in minutes)	
	Two hours	Three hours
Gathering Time with Super Meer	10	10
Bible Story	20	20
Science Time	15	25
Craft Time	15	25
Recreation Time	15	25
Snack Time/Missions	15	25
Music Time	15	25
Reflection Time	15	25

Benefits of Self-Contained VBS:

The classroom is structured to minimize distractions and increase individual attention.

Heroes will get to know and bond with a smaller number of teachers, rather than constantly adjusting to changing teachers and classroom settings.

Benefits of Rotation VBS:

Changing classrooms/stations helps provide a fresh environment for each subject.

Your teachers and volunteers will be able to dive more deeply into each subject/station, and will benefit from short breaks between groups.

What to Expect in Hero Hotline Activity Centers

Bible Beginnings
The activities in Bible Beginnings are useful for helping to welcome and focus your students in the classroom, and/or as an enhancement to your Bible Story and theme-related activities.

Gathering Time
Capture your Heroes' attention using scripts featuring Super Meer and the Professor that are designed to introduce the overall Bible message for each session.

Music Time
Song suggestions, music activities, and rhythm activities will help Heroes connect with themes and Bible stories.

Mission Time
Age-appropriate ideas for mission activities are available in the Mission Leader, available for download at *CokesburyVBS.com*.

Bible Story
Use ideas from "Experience the Bible Story," "Tell the Bible Story," and "Respond to the Bible Story" to immerse your Heroes in the lessons. Help preschoolers and kindergartners learn the Bible Verse and Hotline Tip each day by utilizing the Hero Hotline ASL document found in the Free Resources section at www.cokesburyVBS.com.

Recreation Time
Age-appropriate recreation ideas are listed in this guide as well as in the **Recreation Leader** book.

Craft Time
Heroes will create meaningful reminders of lessons with age-appropriate craft ideas included in this guide.

Science Time
Preschoolers can explore the wonders of creation and reinforce the lessons from each session using these easy-to-follow science experiments.

Snack Time
Create a memorable VBS experience for your children with these fun snacks. Additional recipe ideas for Snack Time are available in the Snack Leader, available for download at *CokesburyVBS.com*.

Reflection Time
Settle down and wrap up each session using ideas in this guide. Use **Bible Activity Stickers**, **Preschool/ Kindergarten Student Books**, and **Younger Elementary Reproducible Fun Pages** to reinforce the session's ideas while Heroes wait for dismissal.

Have even younger children at your VBS? Check out our FREE Toddlers & Twos lessons in the Free Resources section at *CokesburyVBS.com*!

Bible Story

Jesus Builds the Team
John 1:35-51

Hotline Verse

So let's strive for the things that bring peace and the things that build each other up.
(Romans 14:19)

Hotline Tip

Heroes are called to...
Follow Jesus!

Materials
Building Time

- **Hero Hotline Complete Music CD**
- masking or packing tape
- various sizes of boxes
- cardboard blocks

Cave Designs

- large sheet of brown bulletin board paper
- large crayons
- pictures of caves
- masking or painters tape
- baskets or containers

Bible Beginnings

Hero Hotline Manipulatives

During each session, select one or two of these items as arrival activities for the children to use:

- wood or foam puzzles
- large floor puzzles
- lacing cards
- plastic interlocking blocks
- matching card games/activities

Encourage children to work together to complete these activities. Play the song "Let's Strive" as they are working and playing to help them remember the Hotline Verse.

Teamwork Fun
Follow the Leader

Play a simple game of Follow the Leader. Do various fun motions for your group to follow. Once children understand this activity, let them take turns calling out motions for others to follow.

Repeat the Hotline Tip as they play this game.

Curiosity Corner
Building Time

- Before the session, collect several sizes of cardboard boxes.
- Seal the boxes shut using masking or packing tape.
- Add some cardboard blocks.
- Have the children build structures that resemble large caves. Encourage them to help one another stack the boxes and blocks. Repeat the Hotline Verse as they build with boxes and blocks.

Creation Cavern
Cave Designs

- Before the children arrive, crumple up a large sheet of brown bulletin board paper.
- Using masking or painters tape, attach the paper to a wall in one area of your room.
- Show children a few pictures of the insides of colorful caves. Talk with them about making cave drawings on their paper.
- Place colorful large crayons in baskets or containers on the floor.
- Encourage them to create cave drawings on the crumpled-up paper. As they make the cave creations, repeat the theme verse for **Hero Hotline VBS.**

Gathering Time

Professor: (*pacing around with note in hand, notices boys and girls*) **Oh hello, fellow Heroes! I am Professor ____ and I am so glad you have come today. You are just in time. I have been getting lots of phone calls on our hotline asking for help. We work with Heroes around the world to answer all the calls, but we have more calls than we can handle.**

We need more Heroes to work with us. The more Heroes we have helping, the more people we can serve. We're stronger together! Super Meer is coming to help us. This Hero knows all about working together. (*hears crashing noise at the puppet area and investigates*) **Are you OK?**

Super Meer: **Oh, yes. I crash all the time. I'm still working on my flying. I just flew over from Africa.**

Professor: **Oh, are you Super Meer?** (*Super Meer "secretly" hands a paper to Professor.*) **What's this? You want me to read this out loud? To introduce you? OK...** (*clears throat and speaks with "announcer" voice*) **"Who is able to dig tunnels underground? Who is able to leap ant and termite hills in a single bound? Who is always ready to help? It's none other than, Super Meer!"** (*gestures to Super Meer*)

Super Meer: (*pops up*) **Ta-da! Thank you, thank you very much! It is I, Super Meer. I'm here to help.**

Professor: **Yes, thank you Super Meer!** (*pauses, looking intently at Super Meer*) **Super Meer? I hope this doesn't sound rude, but what are you?**

Super Meer: **What am I? I am a superhero, just like all of you.**

Professor: **No, no. I mean, what kind of animal are you?**

Super Meer: **Oh, I'm a meerkat!**

Professor: **Wow, that's amazing. I've never met a talking meerkat.**

Super Meer: **Well, I don't want to brag, but...**

Professor: (*interrupting*) **Anyway, let's get back to our work. There have been so many calls to the hotline that we've had to ask Heroes** (*gestures to audience*) **to help. Could you help us learn how to work together?**

Super Meer: **Well, we meerkats are very good at working as one team. Do you have your Hero Reference Manual?**

Professor: **I sure do.** (*Professor produces a book.*)

Super Meer: **Let's look up "choosing team members."**

Professor: **Aha! It looks like there is a story from the Book of John, chapter one. It tells us how Jesus chose his helpers.**

Super Meer: **I'd like to learn more about this story along with all these Heroes out here. Do you happen to have any sidekicks here at Hero Hotline Headquarters that could help us?**

Professor: **We sure do. Our Sidekicks will be able to tell us more.**

Super Meer: **Great! Let's send these Heroes off to find out more.**

Professor: (*to audience*) **Heroes, up, up, and away to learn more!**

Bible Story
Jesus Builds the Team
John 1:35-51

Hotline Verse
So let's strive for the things that bring peace and the things that build each other up.
(Romans 14:19)

Hotline Tip
Heroes are called to...
Follow Jesus!

Bible Story
Jesus Builds the Team
John 1:35-51

Hotline Verse
So let's strive for the things that bring peace and the things that build each other up.
(Romans 14:19)

Hotline Tip
Heroes are called to...
Follow Jesus!

Materials
Making Drums
•Hero Hotline Craft Theme Stickers
• sturdy paper bowls (2 per child)
• crayons or washable markers
• clean, empty containers (optional idea: baby-wipe containers or oatmeal boxes)
• packing tape
• stapler and staples

Music and Missions Times

Before You Teach
Select the number of songs and activities that will best fit in your available time.

Gather the other necessary items for the music and rhythm activities.

Play the Hero Hotline Complete Music CD as children enter and exit Music Time.

Optional: Make various examples of homemade drums.

Suggested Songs
• "Hero Hotline" (Theme Song)
• "Let's Strive"
• "If U Wanna Be a Hero"

Fun with Music
Sing songs from Hero Hotline Complete Music CD; encourage children to dance and move to the music.

Making Drums
1. Give each child two sturdy paper bowls. Encourage them to add stickers or create hero face shapes with crayons or washable markers on their bowls.

2. Staple the two paper bowls together once the children complete their designs. Or, encourage them to make drums using clean, empty containers such as baby-wipe containers or oatmeal boxes.

3. Seal the sides of the bowls with packing tape is necessary. Make sure the children's names are written on their drums. Play along with songs from the Hero Hotline Complete Music CD.

Music Activity
Play a game of Follow the Leader. Create fun motions for the children to follow. Repeat the Hotline Tip as they play. Ask them to repeat this phrase. Once children have played that game, suggest using their drums as they listen and learn the music.

Encourage them to march around the room while playing their drums to the music.

Rhythm Activity
Begin by suggesting various patterns for children to tap on their drums. Tap a pattern on your drum and have children follow your pattern. After children have caught on to the activity of following a pattern, have them take turns creating their own patterns for the group.

Remind them of the Hotline Tip: Heroes are called to follow Jesus! Ask them to repeat the phrase with you. As a final idea, create a drum pattern for this phrase and ask the children to follow it.

Mission Time
Mission Time will feature several hands-on ideas and options. Check the Mission Leader book (available at *www.cokesburyVBS.com*).

Experience the Bible Story

Transition to the Bible Story

Invite the Heroes to stop their current activity and prepare for the Bible story by joining in this action rhyme.

Who you gonna call?
(*Cup hands around mouth, face front.*)
Who you gonna call?
(*Cup hands around mouth, face to the side.*)
Who you gonna call?
(*Cup hands around mouth, face to the other side.*)
Hero Hotline!
(*Pretend to fly around the room like a superhero.*)

Why?
(*Stop moving. Shrug shoulders.*)

Because Heroes follow Jesus!
(*Sign the name Jesus. Touch your second finger of your right hand to the palm of your left hand. Reverse.*)

Who you gonna call?
(*Cup hands around mouth, face front.*)
Who you gonna call?
(*Cup hands around mouth, face to the side.*)
Who you gonna call?
(*Cup hands around mouth, face to the other side.*)
Hero Hotline!
(*Pretend to fly around the room like a superhero. Stop.*)

Get Ready

Show the children the Bible.

SAY: **This is our Bible. It is a special book that tells us about God and the people who followed God. The Bible has two parts.** (*Turn to Genesis.*) **The Old Testament.**

The Old Testament has stories about many men and women who loved God. (*Turn to Matthew.*) **The second part of our Bible is the New Testament. The New Testament has many stories about Jesus and people who followed Jesus. Today our Bible story is from the New Testament.**

ASK: **What do you remember about Jesus?** (*We celebrate Jesus' birth at Christmas; Jesus is God's Son, Jesus tells us about God, Jesus loves us.*)

SAY: **Today our Bible story is about a time when Jesus was a man. Jesus asked some people to follow him. Let's pretend I'm Jesus. Follow me.**

Place the Bible in your story area.

Have the Heroes line up behind you. Lead the Heroes in a game of Follow the Leader. End the game in your story area.

Imagine the Bible Story

Have the Heroes sit down. Place the Storybook Bible illustration or the Bible Story Poster for Session 1 at child's eye level. Have them gather around the poster or the Bible.

SAY: **Let's use our superhero vision to look at today's story! Look carefully, Heroes. What do you see?**

Invite the Heroes to place their hands around their eyes (like binoculars) and use "hero vision" to see the Bible Story Poster.

Bible Story
Jesus Builds the Team
John 1:35-51

Hotline Verse
So let's strive for the things that bring peace and the things that build each other up.
(Romans 14:19)

Hotline Tip
Heroes are called to...
Follow Jesus!

Materials
Session 1 Bible Story Poster or Bible storybook

Leader Tip
Highlight Genesis and Mark in your Bible ahead of time.

Bible Story
Jesus Builds the Team
John 1:35-51

Hotline Verse
So let's strive for the things that bring peace and the things that build each other up.
(Romans 14:19)

Hotline Tip
Heroes are called to... Follow Jesus!

Leader Tip
Reference the Hero Hotline Sign Language document for all ASL signs.

Tell the Bible Story

SAY: **Listen carefully as I tell the Bible story. Every time I say "Come and see," do what I do.** (*Each time you say "Come and see," make the motion for "come here" and place your hands around your eyes like binoculars.*)

Come and see!
(*Motion: "Come here," Place your hands around your eyes like binoculars.*)

Come and see!
(*Same motion*)

A man named John lived in the desert. People from the cities came to the desert to see John and hear him tell people about God's love.

One day John was talking to two of his friends.

Come and see!
(*Same motion*)

John and his friends saw Jesus walking by.

"Look!" said John. "It is Jesus, God's Son."

John's friends started following Jesus.

"What are you looking for?" asked Jesus.

"Teacher," said the friends. "Where are you staying?"

Jesus said, "Come and see."

Come and see!
(*Same motion*)

One of the two friends was named Andrew. He went to find his brother, Peter.

"I have found Jesus, God's Son," Andrew said to Peter.

Come and see!
(*Same motion*)

Andrew led Peter to Jesus.

The next day Jesus saw a man named Philip.

"Follow me," said Jesus.

Philip found his friend Nathanael.

"I have found Jesus, God's Son," said Philip.

Come and see!
(*Same motion*)

Nathanael went with Philip to meet Jesus.

"Nathanael," said Jesus. "I know all about you. You are good because you never lie or trick people."

Nathanael was surprised. "Jesus," said Nathanael, "You do know all about me. You really are God's Son."

Andrew, Peter, Philip, and Nathanael followed Jesus. They asked other friends to follow Jesus.

We can invite our friends to follow Jesus. We can say,

Come and see!
(*Same motion*)

Come and see!
(*Same motion*)

Show the Bible story poster once again. Respond to the Bible Story
Response Prayer

SAY: Repeat after me:
God, you love us.
And we love you.
Help us follow you
in all that we do.
Amen.

Response Activity

SAY: **In our Bible story today, Jesus chose friends to be a part of his team and follow him. Jesus and his disciples worked together to help many people.**

ASK: **How do you think Andrew, Peter, Philip, and Nathanael felt when they met Jesus?** (*excited, nervous, happy*)

SAY: **Heroes are called to follow Jesus.**

Have the children stand in a circle. Sing the song, "Heroes Are Called" to the tune of "Here We Go Round the Mulberry Bush." Encourage them to march around the circle as they sing.

**Heroes are called to follow Jesus,
Follow Jesus, follow Jesus.
Heroes are called to follow Jesus.
And I'm going to be a hero!**
(*Stop marching. Point to self.*)

Hotline Verse

SAY: **Let's play a game to help us remember our Bible Story.**

Have children sit spaced out in various spots around the room. Walk around and choose one child at a time saying, "Hero _____, follow Jesus!" Have each child then stand up and join the line. Continue around the room and have children help you invite others to follow Jesus. Continue until all children have joined the line, then sit back down in a circle together.

SAY: **We all can follow Jesus, and we all can work together!**

Open the Bible.

SAY: **Our Bible verse is "So let's strive for the things that bring peace and the things that build each other up."**

*Teach the children American Sign Language for the words **peace** and **build**.*

Lead the children in saying the verse again and signing the words.

Bible Story
Jesus Builds the Team
John 1:35-51

Hotline Verse
So let's strive for the things that bring peace and the things that build each other up.
(Romans 14:19)

Hotline Tip
Heroes are called to...
Follow Jesus!

Bible Story

Jesus Builds the Team
John 1:35-51

Hotline Verse

So let's strive for the things that bring peace and the things that build each other up.
(Romans 14:19)

Hotline Tip

Heroes are called to...
Follow Jesus!

Materials

Hero Freeze
• Hero Hotline Complete Music CD
• CD Player

Bring a Friend
• Picture of Jesus (found in the Free Resources section at www. CokesburyVBS.com)

Preschool Recreation

Hero Freeze

Preparation
Make sure the recreation area is safe and ready for play. Cue CD or music tracks and player.

Let's Play!
SAY: **Today we are going to have fun listening to music and moving around.**

At the beginning of the game, I will say "So let's strive together for the things that bring peace and the things that build each other up" (Romans 14:19), and play music. When you hear the music, start singing and moving.

1. While the music plays, move around and have fun.

2. When the music stops, all moving stops and Heroes freeze in place. Encourage them to freeze in a superhero pose.

3. SAY: **"So let's strive together for the things that bring peace and the things that build each other up"** (Romans 14:19), *and play the music again. Play as long as there is interest.*

Bible Tie-in
When you are finished, congratulate the children on being such good Heroes.

SAY: **Heroes are called to follow Jesus. One way we follow Jesus is by learning Bible verses.**

Bring a Friend

Preparation
Make sure the recreation area is safe and ready for play.

Let's Play!
SAY: **When we are followers of Jesus, it's fun to tell our friends about Jesus and invite them to church. Let's pretend to bring our friends to see Jesus.**

1. Have the children choose a friend and go to one side of the room. If you have an uneven number of children, let them make a group of three.

2. Sit on the opposite side of the room from the children. Hold up the picture of Jesus (page 88-89). Give them directions on how to move with their friends across the room to you.

Friend (*child's name*) **and friend** (*child's name*), **hold hands and hop to see Jesus.**

3. Continue the game with other steps like tip-toeing, walking backward, galloping, baby steps, giant steps, and so forth.

Bible Tie-in
When you are finished, congratulate the children on being such good Heroes.

SAY: **Heroes are called to follow Jesus. One way we follow Jesus is by inviting others to "Come and see." We can invite our friends to follow Jesus.**

Cokesbury Craft
Costume Kit

Purpose
To make a visual reminder of being part of the Hero team.

Ages
Appropriate for all ages.

Preparation
- *Cover the tables with tablecloths.*
- *Sort Costume Kit pieces into a bag for each child. Each child needs:*
  - one mask
  - one elastic string
  - two yellow wristbands
  - two purple circles
  - two large green stars
  - two small green stars
  - two orange stars
  - one of each white letters "HERO"
- *As children complete their costume kits, allow them to wear their costumes or place them in the resealable bag with their name on it.*

Directions
Step 1: Peel the back of the sticky side of the "HERO" letters and stars and use them to decorate the mask.

Step 2: Peel the back off and stick the purple circles and large green stars to the wristbands.

Step 3: Tie the elastic string on the mask.

Bible Tie-in
SAY: **Jesus called the disciples to be his hero team. When you wear this costume, remember that you are part of the Hero Hotline team.**
- **How does it make you feel to know that you are a part of God's hero team?**

Bible Story
Jesus Builds the Team
John 1:35-51

Hotline Verse
So let's strive for the things that bring peace and the things that build each other up.
(Romans 14:19)

Hotline Tip
Heroes are called to...
Follow Jesus!

Materials
- **Hero Hotline Tablecloth** or other table covering
- **Costume Kit**
- resealable bags
- permanent marker (for writing names on bags)

Bible Story
Jesus Builds the Team
John 1:35-51

Hotline Verse
So let's strive for the
things that bring peace
and the things that build
each other up.
(Romans 14:19)

Hotline Tip
Heroes are called to...
Follow Jesus!

Materials
- **Hero Hotline Craft
  Theme Stickers**
- paper towel tubes (or
  purchased cardboard
  tubes)
- crayons or markers
- scissors
- paper punch
- colored duct tape
- yarn, string, or
  shoelaces
- permanent markers

Make-It-and-Take-It Bible Craft
Super Vision Binoculars

Purpose
Heroes will use their binoculars when looking at the Bible posters each day.

Ages
Appropriate for all ages. Young Heroes will need assistance.

Preparation
Cut paper towel tubes in half. Each child will need two halves. Or, order cardboard tubes for crafts from Amazon or Walmart. Choose the length you want for the binoculars. Each child will need two tubes the same length.

Cut yarn or string into 18-24" lengths for each child. Wrap a piece of tape around each end of the yarn or string to make the end stiff. Or plan to use shoelaces. This will make the binocular strap.

Directions
1. Give each child two cardboard tubes. Encourage the children to decorate the tubes with crayons, markers, and stickers.

2. Show each child how to hold the two tubes together. Wrap duct tape around the two tubes to hold the binoculars together.

3. Designate one end of the taped tubes as the top. Punch a hole on the outside side of each tube at the top.

4. Give each child the taped yarn or string, or a shoelace. Show the child how to thread the stiff ends of the yarn or shoelaces through the holes at the top of the tubes.

5. Tie a knot in the yarn or shoelace at each hole.

6. Let the children place a Hero sticker on top of the duct tape.

7. Use a permanent marker to write each child's name on their binoculars.

8. Show them how to place the binocular straps over their heads.

SAY: **We can use our binoculars to pretend we have supervision. Let's play a game with our Super Vision Binoculars.**

Play a game of "I Spy" with the children. Hold your binoculars up to your eyes and say, "I spy something (name a color or shape)." Encourage them to hold their binoculars up to their faces and look around the room. Let them guess what you have "spied." Continue the game, letting each child have a turn being the one who says "I spy."

Tip: Use the Super Vision Binoculars with the Bible Story Poster each day.

Bible Story

Jesus Builds the Team
John 1:35-51

Hotline Verse

So let's strive for the things that bring peace and the things that build each other up.
(Romans 14:19)

Hotline Tip

Heroes are called to...
Follow Jesus!

Materials

- magnet wand or large magnet
- a mix of magnetic and non-magnetic items: keys, paper clips, metal washers, screws, magnet tiles; plastic blocks, pens, rubber bands, small toy car
- tape
- cookie sheet or metal tray

Preschool Science
Magnet Play

Preparation

Make a Magnet Sorting Mat.

Use a crayon or marker to make a vertical line down a piece of construction paper to divide the paper in half.

At the top of one side of the paper write "Yes" and draw a happy face. On the other side of the paper write "No" and draw a sad face.

Place the Magnet Sorting Mat and different materials on a table for the children to examine.

Tip: Check items to make sure you have things that are really magnetic. (Not all paper clips are magnetic.) Do not allow the children to place any of the items in their mouths.

Directions

1. Let the children use the magnetic wand or magnet to test each item. If the item is magnetic, place the item on the Yes side of the Magnet Sorting Mat. If the item is not magnetic, place it on the No side of the mat.

2. Place a few of the magnetic items on the cookie sheet. Let the children take turns using the magnetic wand or magnet to make the items "follow" the magnet around the cookie sheet. Try it again using the magnetic wand or magnet on the back of the cookie sheet. Hold the cookie sheet so that the children can get the wand under the sheet.

3. Tape something magnetic onto a small toy car. Let them take turns using the magnetic wand or magnet to make the car move.

What's happening?

Magnets are things that make magnetic fields. The magnetic fields attract metals like iron and make them stick to the magnet.

Bible Connection

SAY: **Jesus did not use magnets to get people to follow him, but we used magnets today to see how things can follow each other. Jesus asked the disciples to follow him so that they could share about God's love for all people. Heroes are called to follow Jesus.**

Preschool Science
Magnet Art

Preparation
Pour washable paint into disposable cups. Cut the paper to fit the bottom of a plastic container.

Directions

1. Have the children wear paint smocks to protect their clothing. Cover the table with tablecloths or paper.

2. Drop the metal items into the paint and use a spoon to remove the items from the paint and drop them into the container on top of the paper.

3. Choose a child to be the "painter." Give the painter the magnetic wand.

4. Hold the plastic tub for the painter. If you have older children, choose two children to hold the tub for the painter.

5. Encourage the painter to place the magnetic wand under the container to move the metal items around.

6. Remove the paper and set it flat to dry.

7. Reset the experiment for the next child.

Bible Connection
When we follow Jesus, just like the magnets moved the objects, we can make beautiful things! When we all work together to bring peace and build each other up, beautiful things can happen!

Bible Story
Jesus Builds the Team
John 1:35-51

Hotline Verse
So let's strive for the things that bring peace and the things that build each other up.
(Romans 14:19)

Hotline Tip
Heroes are called to...
Follow Jesus!

Materials
- **Hero Hotline Tablecloths** or other table coverings
- magnet wand or large magnet
- a mix of magnetic items such as keys, paper clips, metal washers, screws, and magnet tiles
- paper
- scissors
- plastic container
- spoons
- washable paint
- disposable cups
- smocks

Bible Story

Jesus Builds the Team
John 1:35-51

Hotline Verse

So let's strive for the things that bring peace and the things that build each other up.
(Romans 14:19)

Hotline Tip

Heroes are called to...
Follow Jesus!

Ingredients

Simple snacks that can be placed in small bags: crackers, apple slices, gelatin cup and spoon, or cereal mix

Supplies

• resealable snack bags
• napkins
• drink boxes or bags

Snacks
Follow Me Snacks

Have the children follow your directions to collect their own snacks.

Preparation

Place the snack and a napkin in a resealable bag for each child. Place the snack bags in a different room (such as the kitchen). Place the drink boxes or bags in a different room from where you placed the snack bags.

Directions

SAY: **It's snack time. But to get today's snack you have to follow me and do what I do. First, let's say a thank-you prayer.**

Have the children repeat the prayer after you.

PRAY: **Dear God, thank you for good food to eat. Thank you for friends and thank you for Jesus. Amen.**

Have the children line up behind you. Lead them around your room and then to the door, marching with your knees high. Stop at the door.

Start tiptoeing outside your room. Put your finger to your lips and say "Shh!"

After a few minutes, change from tiptoeing to hopping.

Keep changing how you walk as you lead them to the place where you have the snack bags.

When you get to the room with the snack bags, let each child take a bag and then get back in line behind you.

Lead them to the room where you have the drinks. Again, change how you move as you go.

When you get to the room with the drinks, let each child take a drink and then get back in line.

Lead them back to the room where they will eat their snacks.

Have them sit and enjoy their snacks.

SAY: **Heroes, you did a great job following me. Jesus called people to follow him.**

ASK: **What are some things we can do to show we follow Jesus?** (*show love, help others, be kind, share, listen to Bible stories, learn Bible verses, come to VBS*)

Reflection Time

Talk About It
ASK: **Who helps you follow Jesus? Who can you help follow Jesus?**

Prayer
Thank you, God, for Jesus.
Thank you for (*name each teacher and child*)**.**
Amen.

Reflection Time Activity
Have the children sit in a circle.

Teach the children the word work using the sign from American Sign Language.

Teacher: **Heroes are called…**
Children: **to follow Jesus**
All: **I want to be a Hero!**
(*Have the children hold out their arms like they are flying.*)

Go to each child and give them a **Scripture Treasure Lanyard** and the **Session 1 sticker.**

SAY: **Hero** (*child's name*)**, you are called to follow Jesus.**

SAY: **Our Bible verse is "So let's strive for the things that bring peace and the things that build each other up."**

Teach the children American Sign Language for the words **peace,** *and* **build,** *and* **up.**

Lead the children in saying the verse again and signing the three words.

Bible Story
Jesus Builds the Team
John 1:35-51

Hotline Verse
So let's strive for the things that bring peace and the things that build each other up.
(Romans 14:19)

Hotline Tip
Heroes are called to…
Follow Jesus!

Supplies
• **Scripture Treasure Lanyards** and **Session 1 Stickers**

Leader Tip
Reference the Hero Hotline Sign Language document for all ASL signs.

Bible Story

Shiphrah, Puah, and Miriam: God's Wonder Women
Exodus 1:8–2:10

Hotline Verse

So let's strive for the things that bring peace and the things that build each other up.
(Romans 14:19)

Hotline Tip

Heroes are called to... Help Others!

Materials
Helping Others

- **Hero Hotline Craft Theme Stickers**
- adhesive bandages
- gauze
- cotton balls
- child-size first-aid kits

Cave Fossils

- soft modeling clay
- small plastic toy animals
- small plastic bug shapes
- waxed paper
- pictures of the insides of caves

Creating Cards

- used greeting cards
- colorful construction paper
- watercolor paints
- washable markers

Bible Beginnings

Hero Hotline Manipulatives

During each session, select one or two of these items as arrival activities for the children:

- wood or foam puzzles
- large floor puzzles
- lacing cards
- plastic interlocking blocks
- matching card games/activities

Encourage children to work together to complete these activities. Repeat the theme verse as they play together.

Teamwork Fun
Helping Others

Provide children with child-size first-aid kits. Encourage them to role-play helping others who are sick or hurt. Remind them of the Hotline Tip. Talk about ways to help others.

Curiosity Corner
Cave Fossils

- Cover the area with waxed paper.
- Set out various plastic toy shapes and colors of soft modeling clay.
- Display pictures of the insides of caves.

Talk with the children about creating fossil shapes that can be found in caves. Encourage them to create various fossil shapes using the clay and plastic shapes. As they create their shapes, ask them repeat the theme verse with you.

Creation Cavern
Creating Cards for Others

Let children make cards of encouragement for others. As children complete their cards, remind them of their Hotline Tip. Talk about ways they are helping others by making the cards.

Tip: Have cards with pre-written messages for children to copy.

Gathering Time

Professor: (*finishing up a call in the phone booth*) **Yes, Mother. I ate breakfast this morning. And, I brushed my teeth. Yes, I even exercised.** (*notices audience*) **Oh Mom, I have to go. I'll call you later. I love you.** (*emerges from phone booth*)

Hello fellow Heroes! I'm am so glad to see you back today! That was my mother. She calls the hotline from time to time to check on me. She really loves me. (*crashing sound and Super Meer pops up with something hanging on his head*) **Are you OK, Super Meer?**

Super Meer: **Oh yes. I'm still working on flying. Did I hear you say your mom calls the hotline? That's great. I still see my mom every day.**

Professor: **Really? Even with your busy hero schedule?**

Super Meer: **Oh, yes. I always have time for my "mob." I fly home each day to my mob.**

Professor: **Your mob?**

Super Meer: **That's what you call a group of meerkats. It's not a very big one. There are only ten of us.**

Professor: **There are ten in your family? That sounds pretty big.**

Super Meer: **That's nothing. There can be as many as 40 meerkats living in a mob at a time. The Carrot mob, just past the water hole, has 37 meerkats.**

Professor: **Carrot mob?**

Super Meer: **It's what I call the family next door. They really like carrots. By the way, do you know what you call a meerkat with carrots in its ears?**

Professor: **No, what?**

Super Meer: **Whatever you want. She or he can't hear you anyway.** (*laughing*) **No, seriously, they are a really nice family. They have a great leader. She's a super matriarch.**

Professor: **What's a matriarch?**

Super Meer: **It's what we call the female meerkat who is in charge of a mob. For humans, it's a woman who is the leader of her family. In my mob, the matriarch is my mom. She's great at helping others.**

Professor: (*pulls out book*) **We've had a lot of calls lately about needing helpers. I wonder if there are any stories about women helpers in our Hero Reference Manual?**

Super Meer: **Let's take a look.**

Professor: (*pulls out book*) **Here's one. "Wonder Women Help Save Babies."**

Super Meer: **Wow! I think our Heroes need to hear that story.**

Bible Story
Shiphrah, Puah, and Miriam: God's Wonder Women
Exodus 1:8–2:10

Hotline Verse
So let's strive for the things that bring peace and the things that build each other up.
(Romans 14:19)

Hotline Tip
Heroes are called to... Help Others!

Professor: **I think so too, but first think we should start with our Hotline Verse. Some of these Heroes may remember it from last time. Let's see if we can say it again. It comes from Romans 14:19. "So, let's strive for the things that bring peace and the things that build each other up."**

Super Meer: **I think it's time to head out with our Sidekicks, so here's a hotline tip to take with you: Heroes are called to help others!**

Professor: **Heroes, up, up, and away to learn more!**

Music and Missions Times

Before You Teach
• Select the number of songs and activities that will best fit your available time.

• Gather the necessary items for the music and rhythm activities.

• Play the Hero Hotline Complete Music CD as the children enter and exit Music Time.

Suggested Songs
• "Hero Hotline" (Theme Song)
• "If U Wanna Be a Hero"
• "Hold Up"

Fun with Music
Use a variety of simple rhythm instruments for this activity.

1. Assist children as they select an instrument to play.

2. Play several songs from the Hero Hotline Complete Music CD.

3. Encourage children to play their instruments.

After a couple of songs have been played, ask them to trade instruments with others in the class.

Remind children of the Bible story and the theme verse. As they trade and share instruments, remind them they are helping others to live in peace and be kind to one another.

Rhythm Activity
SAY: **It is so fun to make rhythms with our instruments! Let's see if we can remember the rhythms we played as we rhythm paint!**

Place a small amount of paint in small bowls. Make sure the names of the children are on their papers.

Help children attach a pom-pom to a clothespin.

Remind them of the Hotline Tip for this session and ways we can help others.

Show them how to place the pom-pom in the paint and then onto the construction paper. Use a variety of musical sounds and patterns.

Ask them to follow those sounds and paint with their pom-poms as they hear various rhythms.

Mission Time
Mission Time will feature several hands-on ideas and options. Look in the Mission Leader book (*available at www.cokesburyVBS.com*) and select the options that best fit the needs of your church.

Bible Story
Shiphrah, Puah, and Miriam: God's Wonder Women
Exodus 1:8–2:10

Hotline Verse
So let's strive for the things that bring peace and the things that build each other up.
(Romans 14:19)

Hotline Tip
Heroes are called to... Help Others!

Materials
Fun with Music
• **Hero Hotline Complete Music CD**
• simple rhythm instruments

Rhythm Activity
• pom-poms (one per child)
• clothespins (one per child)
• construction paper
• tempera paint
• small bowls
• marker (adult use)

Bible Story

Shiphrah, Puah, and Miriam: God's Wonder Women
Exodus 1:8–2:10

Hotline Verse

So let's strive for the things that bring peace and the things that build each other up.
(Romans 14:19)

Hotline Tip

Heroes are called to...
Help Others!

Materials

- **Session 2 Bible Story Poster** or Bible Storybook
- **Super Vision Binoculars** from Session 1

Leader Tips

- Reference the Hero Hotline Sign Language document for all ASL signs.

- You can add texture to your "river" by letting the children glue on torn pieces of tissue paper or construction paper.

Experience the Bible Story

Transition to the Bible Story

Invite the Heroes to stop their current activity and prepare for the Bible story by joining in this action rhyme.

Who you gonna call?
(*Cup hands around mouth, face front.*)
Who you gonna call?
(*Cup hands around mouth, face to the side.*)
Who you gonna call?
(*Cup hands around mouth, face to the other side.*)
Hero Hotline!
(*Pretend to fly around the room like a superhero.*)
Why?
(*Stop moving. Shrug shoulders.*)
Because Heroes help others!
(*Sign the word **help** in American Sign Language. Hold out your left hand palm up. Place your right fist with thumb pointing up in the left palm. Move both hands up.*)

Who you gonna call?
(*Cup hands around mouth, face front.*)
Who you gonna call?
(*Cup hands around mouth, face to the side.*)
Who you gonna call?
(*Cup hands around mouth, face to the other side.*)
Hero Hotline!
(*Pretend to fly around the room like a superhero. Stop.*)

Get Ready

(*Show the children the Bible.*)

SAY: **This is our Bible. It is a special book that tells us about God and the people who followed God. The Bible has two parts.** (*Turn to Genesis.*) **The Old Testament. The Old Testament has stories**

about many men and women who loved God. (*Turn to Matthew.*) **The second part of our Bible is the New Testament. The New Testament has many stories about Jesus and people who followed Jesus.** (*Turn to Exodus.*) **Today our Bible story is from the Old Testament. It's about some women who helped a baby named Moses.** (*Place the Bible in your story area.*) **Now I need your help. I want you to help me make a pretend river. We will sit around the river as I tell you the story.**

(*Place a long piece of blue mural paper on the floor of your story area.*)

SAY: **This will be our pretend river. You can help by coloring the river with crayons.**

(*Have the children use crayons to decorate the paper. Thank the Heroes for their help.*)

Imagine the Bible Story

Have the Heroes sit down around the paper river. Place the Bible Storybook page or the poster for Session 2 at child's eye level. If you chose to make the Super Vision Binoculars in Session 1, give the Heroes their binoculars.

SAY: **Let's use our superhero vision to look at today's Bible story! Look carefully, Heroes. What do you see?**

Invite the Heroes to look through their binoculars or place their hands around their eyes. Encourage them to use "hero vision" to see the Bible story.

SAY: **I wonder what's happening in this picture?**

Tell the Bible Story

Teach the children the ASL sign for "help." Make a fist with one hand with your thumb up. Bring your other hand, palm facing up underneath the fist hand and raise both hands.

SAY: **Listen carefully as I tell the Bible story. Every time I say "help" make the sign I just taught you.**

Help, help, help!
(*Sign "help."*)

Many years ago there was a group of people called the Hebrews. The Hebrews loved God. They had moved to Egypt, a country far away. For a while, the Hebrews were happy in Egypt. But when a new king became ruler in Egypt, the Hebrews were unhappy.

The king of Egypt was called Pharaoh. He was a mean king. He was unkind to the Hebrews and made them work very hard. He did not want the Hebrews to have any baby boys. Pharaoh made a rule that all boy babies born to the Hebrews were to be killed. Girl babies could live.

So the Hebrews asked God for…

Help, help, help!
(*Sign "help."*)

Two Hebrew women became God's helpers. Their names were Shiphrah and Puah. Those are hard names to say! So let's practice. (*Use pronunciation key.*)

Shiphrah and Puah had special jobs. They took care of the mothers and babies when the babies were born. They did not do what Pharaoh said to do. Shiprah

and Puah let the boys live.

One baby boy was named Moses. When Moses was born, Moses' mother knew her baby was still in danger from the Pharaoh. Moses' mother needed…

Help, help, help!
(*Sign "help."*)

Moses' sister became God's helper. Her name was Miriam. Moses' mother laid baby Moses in a basket and put the basket in the river behind some tall grasses. Miriam also hid in the grasses. She watched over her baby brother. Miriam kept baby Moses safe.

One of the pharaoh's daughters came to the river. The princess saw the baby and picked him up.

When Miriam saw what was happening, she ran to the princess. "Would you like me to get a woman to take care of the baby?" she asked.

"Yes," said the princess. "Go and get someone."

Miriam ran to get Moses' mother and brought her to the princess.

Baby Moses was now safe in the care of his mother and the princess.

Moses grew to be a man. He knew that the Hebrews needed…

Help, help, help!
(*Sign "help."*)

Moses became God's helper.

Bible Story
Shiphrah, Puah, and Miriam: God's Wonder Women
Exodus 1:8–2:10

Hotline Verse
So let's strive for the things that bring peace and the things that build each other up.
(Romans 14:19)

Hotline Tip
Heroes are called to… Help Others!

Leader Tip
Reference the Hero Hotline Sign Language document for all ASL signs.

Pronunciation Key:
Shiphrah = Shiff-rah
Puah = Pooh-ah.

Bible Story

Shiphrah, Puah, and Miriam: God's Wonder Women
Exodus 1:8–2:10

Hotline Verse

So let's strive for the things that bring peace and the things that build each other up.
(Romans 14:19)

Hotline Tip

Heroes are called to...
Help Others!

Materials

• **Session 2 Bible Story Poster** or storybook Bible.

Respond to the Bible Story

Response Prayer

SAY: **Repeat after me.**
God, we can help our neighbors.
We can help our friends.
Help us always remember.
Your love never ends.
Amen.

Response Activity

Show the Bible Story Poster or Bible storybook illustration again.

ASK: **How do you think the women felt when they helped baby Moses?**

SAY: **Heroes are called to help others.**

Have the children stand in a circle. Sing the song, "Heroes Are Called" to the tune of "Here We Go Round the Mulberry Bush." Encourage them to march around the circle as they sing.

Heroes are called to help each other, help each other, help each other.
Heroes are called to help each other.
And I'm going to be a hero!
(*Stop marching. Point to self.*)

Hotline Verse

Open the Bible.

SAY: **Our Bible verse is "So let's strive for the things that bring peace and the things that build each other up."**

Teach the children American Sign Language for the words *peace* and *build*.

Lead them in saying the verse again and signing the words.

Preschool Recreation

Help Baby Moses

Preparation
Make sure the recreation area is safe and ready for play.

Let's Play!
SAY: **Miriam was God's helper. She watched over Moses to keep him safe.**

1. Have the Heroes sit on the floor.
2. Choose a child to pretend to be Miriam. Have Miriam go outside of the room with another teacher. Or have Miriam cover her or his eyes with both hands.
3. Hide the baby doll somewhere in the room.
4. Have Miriam come back in the room or uncover his or her eyes.
5. Let Miriam look for the baby doll. The remaining children will shout "Closer!" when Miriam moves close to the doll, or shout "Farther!" when Miriam moves away from the doll.
6. When Miriam finds the doll, the children shout, "Heroes are called to help others!"
7. Repeat the game until everyone has been Miriam (including the boys!).

Bible Tie-in
When you are finished, congratulate the children on being such good Heroes.

SAY: **Heroes are called to help others.**

It's Time to Help

Preparation
Make sure the recreation area is safe and ready for play.

Let's Play!
1. Have the children move to an open area of the room.
2. Start the game with you or another leader as the Hero. Have the Hero stand on one side of the room, facing the other side of the room.
3. Have the rest of the children stand on the opposite side of the room, facing the Hero.

SAY: **Let's play a game, "It's Time to Help." All of you except the Hero will ask, "What time is it, Hero?" The Hero will say a time like "It's two o'clock." You will each move two steps forward. Then you will ask the question again. The Hero will tell you another time and you will move forward that many steps. If the Hero says, "It's time to help!" you must turn around and run back to your side of the room. The Hero will chase you and try to tag you.**

Tip: Help the children play the game. If you have older children, let younger children take turns being the Hero.

Bible Tie-in
SAY: **In our Bible story today, some women were God's helpers. They helped keep baby Moses safe.**

Bible Story
Shiphrah, Puah, and Miriam: God's Wonder Women
Exodus 1:8–2:10

Hotline Verse
So let's strive together for the things that bring peace and the things that build each other up. (Romans 14:19)

Hotline Tip
Heroes are called to... Help Others!

Materials

Help Baby Moses
• baby doll

Bible Story

Shiphrah, Puah, and Miriam: God's Wonder Women
Exodus 1:8–2:10

Hotline Verse

So let's strive together for the things that bring peace and the things that build each other up. (Romans 14:19)

Hotline Tip

Heroes are called to... Help Others!

Materials

- **Hero Hotline Tablecloth** or other table covering
- **Air Clay with Accessories kit**
- paper plates
- pens, pencils, or markers

Cokesbury Craft

Air Clay Heroes

Purpose

To create a reminder to live out the Hotline Verse in our daily lives.

Ages

Appropriate for all ages.

Preparation

- Cover the tables with tablecloths.
- Place a (closed) bag of clay of each color, an orange cape, and a purple mask on a paper plate for each Hero. Write each Hero's name on the paper plate.

Directions

Step 1: Mold the clay into various shapes to create a hero or hero team. Alternatively, have the Heroes work in teams to create a team of Heroes. Use the mask and cape to provide accessories to one or more of your Heroes.

Step 2: Set molded figures aside to dry.

Step 3: Play! Use the molded creations to tell stories of God's Heroes!

Bible Tie-in

SAY: **God calls us to work together as Heroes.**
- **What special skills do your Heroes have?**

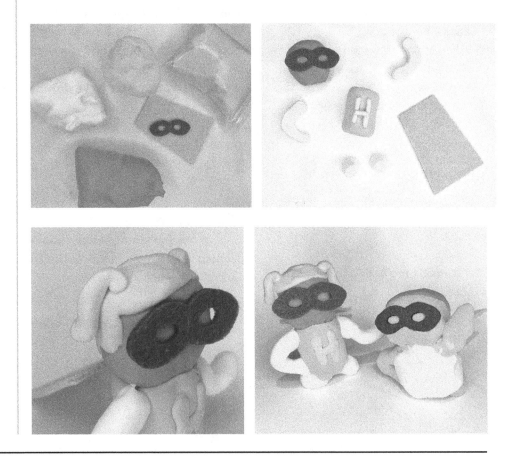

Make-It-and-Take-It Bible Craft
Bag Basket

Purpose
Heroes will make a basket to remind them of the Bible story.

Preparation
Cut off the top half of a lunch bag for each child. This will make a basket about 4-5" deep. Save the paper from the tops of the bags.

Tear masking tape into short strips. Tape one end of several strips to the edge of the table at each child's place.

Directions
1. Give each child the bottom half of the bag and several strips of tape.

2. Let the children pull up the strips and tape them onto the bottom half of the bag.

3. Give each child the top part of the bag. Let them tear the paper into smaller strips.

4. Encourage the children to glue the torn paper strips onto the outside of the basket bag.

SAY: **In our Bible story, many women were helpers. Shiphrah and Puah helped as babies were born. Moses' mother put baby Moses in a basket to hide him. Moses' sister watched over the baby. A princess found baby Moses and kept him safe as he grew.**

Bible Story
Shiphrah, Puah, and Miriam: God's Wonder Women
Exodus 1:8–2:10

Hotline Verse
So let's strive for the things that bring peace and the things that build each other up.
(Romans 14:19)

Hotline Tip
Heroes are called to... Help Others!

Materials
Bag Basket
• lunch-size paper bags
• masking tape
• glue

Bible Story

Shiphrah, Puah, and Miriam: God's Wonder Women
Exodus 1:8–2:10

Hotline Verse

So let's strive for the things that bring peace and the things that build each other up.
(Romans 14:19)

Hotline Tip

Heroes are called to... Help Others!

Materials
Baby Moses

- cardboard tubes
- glue sticks
- scissors
- tissue paper or fabric scraps
- crayons or markers

I Can Help Coupons

- Coupons Template (found in the Free Resources section at www.CokesburyVBS.com)
- scissors
- crayons or markers

Make-It-and-Take-It Craft

Baby Moses

Purpose

Heroes will make a reminder of the Bible story.

Preparation

Use purchased cardboard craft tubes (available at Amazon and Walmart) or cut paper towel tubes into 4" lengths for each child.

Directions

1. Give each child a cardboard tube. Show the children how to use the glue stick to spread glue all over the tube.

2. Help the children place pieces of tissue paper or fabric scraps over the glue to cover the tubes. This will make baby Moses' blanket.

3. Let them use crayons or markers to draw a happy face at one end of the tubes. This will make baby Moses' face.

4. Place baby Moses in the paper bag basket.

I Can Help Coupons

Purpose

Coupons will remind Heroes to help others.

Preparation

Photocopy and cut out the Coupons Template for each child.

Directions

1. Give each child the coupons. Let the children decorate the coupons with crayons or markers.

2. Read the coupons to the children.

SAY: **Take your baskets home. Pick out a coupon each day to find a way to help your family.**

Preschool Science
Sink or Float

Preparation
Partially fill a plastic tub or water table with water. Give each child a clear plastic glass partially filled with water. Set out the items that will sink or float.

Directions
1. Show the children the items. Let them choose an item.

ASK: **Do you think this item will sink or float?**

2. Choose a child to drop the item into the water tub or table. What happens?

3. Give each child the item to drop into her or his glass.

4. Continue encouraging them to test each item by dropping into their glasses.

SAY: **In our Bible story, Moses' mother wanted to keep baby Moses safe from the pharaoh. So she put him in a basket and placed him in a river.**

ASK: **Do you think the basket floated on the water?**

SAY: **Let's see what happens when we try to float a basket.**

5. Drop the basket into the water. The basket will eventually sink. You may need to make "waves" to sink the basket.

SAY: **Oh no! The basket sank. But Moses' basket did not sink.**

ASK: **Why do you think the basket floated?**

SAY: **The Bible tells us that Moses' mother painted the basket with something called tar. The tar made it so no water could seep into the basket. It made the basket float.**

What's Happening?
If we could use our supervision to look deep inside each thing we used in our experiment today we would see molecules. Everything in the whole world is made of molecules. Molecules are too tiny to see with our eyes, but they are there.

If the molecules in something are squished tightly together, the thing will sink. A rock has molecules squished together so it sinks. If the molecules in something are more spread out, the thing will float. A piece of wood has molecules that are spread out so it will float.

Bible Story
Shiphrah, Puah, and Miriam: God's Wonder Women
Exodus 1:8–2:10

Hotline Verse
So let's strive for the things that bring peace and the things that build each other up.
(Romans 14:19)

Hotline Tip
Heroes are called to... Help Others!

Materials:
Sink or Float
- water
- plastic tub or water table
- clear plastic drinking glasses for each child items that will sink such as keys, coins, toy cars, and rocks; items that float such as small rubber balls, foam shapes, bathtub toys, crayons, and plastic blocks
- a small basket

Bible Story

Shiphrah, Puah, and Miriam: God's Wonder Women
Exodus 1:8–2:10

Hotline Verse

So let's strive for the things that bring peace and the things that build each other up.
(Romans 14:19)

Hotline Tip

Heroes are called to... Help Others!

Materials
Make a River

• aluminum foil
• water
• sand

Preschool Science
Make a River

Preparation

Tear off a long piece of aluminum foil. Fold the foil in half lengthwise.

Directions

1. Place the folded aluminum foil on the ground. Let the Heroes shape the foil into a curvy, snake-like shape.

2. Let them press sand around the edge of the foil.

3. Let the children help you build up one end of the foil with dirt so that this end is higher than the other end.

4. Pour water in the higher end and watch it run.

Tips: Do this activity outside or in a water or sand table. For extra fun, add blue food coloring to your water.

Have towels to wipe up spills and dry hands.

What's Happening?

Water in a river moves because of gravity. Gravity makes everything pull towards the center of the earth. Gravity is why we don't float in the air.

Snacks

Moses in the Blanket

Note: This snack is not recommended for children under the age of 4 due to choking hazards.

Preparation
Preheat oven to 375 degrees.

Directions
1. Cut the hotdogs in half.

2. Open the crescent rolls can and separate the triangles.

3. Wrap a triangle around each hotdog half.

4. Place the wrapped dog on a baking sheet.

5. Bake at 375 for about 10-15 minutes or until golden brown.

6. Place the wrapped hot dog in a cupcake liner.

SAY: **Our snack today reminds me of our Bible story. It's baby Moses in his basket.**

Float Moses in the River

Preparation
Make blue gelatin according to the directions on the package. Pour the gelatin into clear plastic cups for each child.

Directions
1. Give each child a cup of blue gelatin.

SAY: **Let's pretend this cup is filled with water from a river. In our Bible story Moses' mother put baby Moses in a basket and then placed him in a river. His sister Miriam watched over him to make sure he was safe. Let's put a pretend baby Moses in the river.**

2. Give each child a gummy bear to represent baby Moses. Let the children "float" baby Moses on the river.

3. Give each child a spoon and napkin. Enjoy today's snack.

Bible Story
Shiphrah, Puah, and Miriam: God's Wonder Women
Exodus 1:8–2:10

Hotline Verse
So let's strive for the things that bring peace and the things that build each other up.
(Romans 14:19)

Hotline Tip
Heroes are called to... Help Others!

Materials
Moses in the Blanket
- oven
- hot dogs
- crescent rolls
- baking sheet
- knife (adult use only)
- cupcake liners

Float Moses in the River
- blue gelatin
- gummy bears
- clear plastic cups
- spoons
- napkin
- mixing bowl
- mixing spoon
- measuring cups

Bible Story

Shiphrah, Puah, and Miriam: God's Wonder Women
Exodus 1:8–2:10

Hotline Verse

So let's strive for the things that bring peace and the things that build each other up.
(Romans 14:19)

Hotline Tip

Heroes are called to...
Help Others!

Materials

• Scripture Treasure Lanyards and Session 2 Stickers

Reflection Time

Talk About It

ASK: **Who are Heroes in our community?** (*doctors, nurses, police, firefighters, pastors*) **Who is a hero in your life?**

Prayer

Thank you, God for people who help. Thank you for (*name each teacher and child*).
Amen.

Reflection Activity

Have the children sit in a circle.

Teach the children the word help using the ASL sign.

Teacher: **Heroes are called...**
Children: **to help others**
All: **I want to be a Hero!**
(*Have the children hold out their arms like they are flying.*)

Go to each child and give a Session 2 sticker for their Scripture Treasure Lanyard.

SAY: **Hero** (*child's name*) **you are called to help others.**

Our Bible verse is "So let's strive together for the things that bring peace and the things that build each other up."

Teach the children American Sign Language for the words *together*, *peace*, and *build*.

Lead the children in saying the verse again and signing the three words.

Bible Beginnings

Hero Hotline Manipulatives

During each session, select one or two of these items as arrival activities for the children:

- wood or foam puzzles
- large floor puzzles
- lacing cards
- plastic interlocking blocks
- matching card games/activities

Encourage children to work together to complete these activities. Repeat the theme verse as they play together.

Teamwork Fun
I Can Be a Helper

- Use masking tape to create a start and finish line on the floor or ground. Lines need to be about 12-15 feet apart.

- Make sure each child has a partner or a group of four to play this game. Have each child hold one end of the towel. Place the ball in the middle of the towel.

- The goal for each pair is to see if they can go from the starting line to the finish line without dropping the ball. The goal is to work together to keep the focus on the ball. Repeat the theme verse as the game is being played.

SAY: **Heroes are called to work together!**

Curiosity Corner
Compass Time

- Tell the Heroes to pretend they are in a large cave. Using a large compass, show children how a compass moves and tells them which direction they are going. Explain the letters: N stands for North, S stands for South, and so on. Let them hold the compass and experiment: walking in different directions and watching the compass needle move.

SAY: **We can all follow God and work together at Hero Hotline!**

Creation Cavern
Hero Friends

- Suggest children use the chenille stems to create hero shapes. Have each child team up with other children to create these shapes.

- Show them how to bend the stems into different shapes.

- Talk with them about what shapes they are making.

- Repeat the theme verse as they create their designs. Ask them to repeat the verse.

- Display these shapes for all to see.

Bible Story
Jethro Mentors Moses
Exodus 18

Hotline Verse
So let's strive for the things that bring peace and the things that build each other up.
(Romans 14:19)

Hotline Tip
Heroes are called to... Work Together!

Materials
I Can Be a Helper
- plastic ball
- towels (one towel for two children)
- masking tape
- large compass

Hero Friends
- chenille stems
- markers for the teachers

Safety tip
Fold down the tips of the stems if they are too pointy or scratchy.

Bible Story

Jethro Mentors Moses
Exodus 18

Hotline Verse

So let's strive for the things that bring peace and the things that build each other up. (Romans 14:19)

Hotline Tip

Heroes are called to...
Work Together!

Gathering Time

Professor: **Welcome back, Heroes! I'm so glad you are here. It's been a busy day so far. I took out the trash and replaced five light bulbs. Then, I realized that someone or something has been digging around here and cut the phone lines. So, I repaired the phones. Once the phones were up and running again, I received 15 new distress calls and responded to all of them. Phew!** (*wipes forehead*) **There is so much to do. Have you seen Super Meer?**

Super Meer: (*pops up, acting as if chewing*) **Hello fellow Heroes! I'm sorry I'm late. I was doing some digging today. By the way, I think I noticed a few light bulbs out. You may want to replace those. And I think I heard the phone ringing a few times.**

Professor: (*exasperated*) **You did all that?**

Super Meer: **Yes, I've been busy today. What have you been doing?**

Professor: **Oh, just some clean up after a certain superhero.**

Super Meer: (*clears throat*) **Uh-hmm. Then shouldn't we be getting back to work?**

Professor: **Yes, absolutely.** (*enters phone booth*) **Hello, Hero Hotline. How can we be of assistance today? Uh-huh. Yes, hello Super Mom. Uh-huh...**(*continues to "talk" silently on phone*)

Super Meer: (*to audience*) **Wow, Super Mom... I'm sure you've heard of her. She is that Super-Mom that has four arms. She really**

does have eyes in the back of her head. She has the superpower of being able to do 20 things at the same time. This woman is incredible!

Professor: (*finishing up call*) **Yes, ma'am. Don't worry. We will get right on this.** (*exits booth*) **Wow, she sure needs help. She said that she loves helping people, but she has so much to do she can't seem to keep up with all the emergencies there.**

Super Meer: **Whoa! And, I thought I was busy with my digging. If Super Mom can't keep up, then she must be super busy. We do need to help her out.**

Professor: **Agreed. Let's look in the Hero Reference Manual.**

Super Meer: **Look for something about too much work.**

Professor: (*looking through book*): **Aha! This story can help. It's about a time when an important leader named Moses was trying to do too many things by himself.**

Super Meer: **Well, we need to learn more about what he did. I'm sure I have a Hotline Tip that can help us.**

Professor: **Let's remember two of our Hotline Tips: 1. Heroes are called to follow Jesus. 2. Heroes are called help others. Do you remember the hand motions?** (*Demonstrate and repeat.*)

Super Meer: **Perhaps we should recite the Hotline Verse, too!**

Professor: **Perfect! Let's say it together. It's from Romans 14:19, "So, let's strive for the things that bring peace and the things that build each other up."** (*Demonstrate hand motions as necessary.*) **OK Heroes, up, up, and away...**

Super Meer: (*interrupting*) **Wait! I just remembered! The Hotline Tip for today is Heroes are called to work together!**

Professor: **Good job, Super Meer! Let's say today's tip together. Heroes are called to work together!**

Super Meer: **I'm glad I remembered it in time!**

Professor: **Yes, me too. Let's try this again. Heroes, up, up, and away to learn more!**

Bible Story
Jethro Mentors Moses
Exodus 18

Hotline Verse
So let's strive for the things that bring peace and the things that build each other up.
(Romans 14:19)

Hotline Tip
Heroes are called to...
Work Together!

Bible Story
Jethro Mentors Moses
Exodus 18

Hotline Verse
So let's strive for the things that bring peace and the things that build each other up.
(Romans 14:19)

Hotline Tip
Heroes are called to...
Work Together!

Materials
Hero Movement
- **Hero Hotline Complete Music CD**
- crepe paper (purple, red, and blue)
- masking tape
- scissors (adult use)
- marker (adult use)
- plastic shower curtain rings

Rhythm Activity
- kitchen pots and pans
- short-handled wooden spoons

Music and Missions Times

Before You Teach
Select the number of songs and activities that will best fill in your available time.

Gather the necessary items for the music and rhythm activities.

Play the Hero Hotline Complete Music CD as the children enter and exit Music Time.

Suggested Songs
- "Hero Hotline" (Theme Song)
- "Work Together"
- "If U Wanna Be a Hero"

Fun with Music
Hero Movement

1. Before the children arrive, pre-cut crepe paper streamer into 12" strips.

2. Help them add masking tape to their streamers. Next, help them attach the streamers to shower curtain rings. Add a piece of masking tape with the name of each child on their shower curtain ring.

3. Remind children of the theme verse and Hotline Tip. Talk about ways they can work together to be kind and helpful and bring peace to one another.

4. Play several songs from the Hero Hotline Complete Music CD. Encourage the children to move to the music and wave their streamers as they music is being played.

Rhythm Activity
Hand out pots and pans. Ask the children to beat on the bottoms of the pots and pans with the short-handled wooden spoons. Tell them they are part of a hero band. Remind them of their Hotline Tip and how they are working together as a band.

Mission Time
Mission Time will feature hands-on ideas. There are several options. Look in the Mission Leader book and select the options that best fit your church's needs.

Experience the Bible Story

Transition to the Bible Story

Invite the Heroes to stop their current activity and prepare for the Bible story by joining in this action rhyme:

Who you gonna call?
(*Cup hands around mouth, face front.*)
Who you gonna call?
(*Cup hands around mouth, face to the side.*)
Who you gonna call?
(*Cup hands around mouth, face to the other side.*)
Hero Hotline!
(*Pretend to fly around the room like a superhero.*)
Why?
(*Stop moving. Shrug shoulders.*)
Because Heroes work together!
(*Sign the word together.*)

Who you gonna call?
(*Cup hands around mouth, face front.*)
Who you gonna call?
(*Cup hands around mouth, face to the side.*)
Who you gonna call?
(*Cup hands around mouth, face to the other side.*)
Hero Hotline!
(*Pretend to fly around the room like a superhero. Stop.*)

Get Ready

Show the children the Bible.

SAY: **This is our Bible. It is a special book that tells us about God and the people who followed God. The Bible has two parts.** (*Turn to Genesis.*) **The Old Testament. The Old Testament has stories about many men and women who loved God.** (*Turn to Matthew.*) **The second part of our Bible is** the New Testament. **The New Testament has many stories about Jesus and people who followed Jesus. Today our Bible story is from the Old Testament.** (*Turn to Exodus.*) **It's another story about Moses. In this story Moses is no longer a baby. He grew and grew and grew. Now Moses is a man.** (*Place the Bible in your story area.*)

You are growing just like baby Moses grew. When you were a baby, you had to take baby steps. Let's take baby steps to our story area. (*Have the children take baby steps for a few minutes.*) **Stop! Now that you have grown bigger you can take giant steps.** (*Have them take giant steps until they reach the story area.*)

Imagine the Bible Story

Have the Heroes sit down. Place the Bible Story Poster or Storybook Bible at child's eye level. If you chose to make the Super Vision Binoculars, give each child their binoculars.

SAY: **Let's use our superhero vision to look at today's story poster! Look carefully, Heroes. What do you see?**

Invite the Heroes to look through the binoculars or place their hands around their eyes (like binoculars). Encourage them to use their "hero vision" to see the Bible Story Poster.

SAY: **I wonder what's happening in this picture? What do you think the people are doing?**

Bible Story
Jethro Mentors Moses
Exodus 18

Hotline Verse
So let's strive for the things that bring peace and the things that build each other up.
(Romans 14:19)

Hotline Tip
Heroes are called to...
Work Together!

Materials
- **Session 3 Bible Story Poster** or storybook Bible
- **Super Vision Binoculars** from Session 1

Bible Story
Jethro Mentors Moses
Exodus 18

Hotline Verse
So let's strive for the things that bring peace and the things that build each other up.
(Romans 14:19)

Hotline Tip
Heroes are called to...
Work Together!

Materials
• Session 3 Bible Story **Poster** or storybook Bible

Tell the Bible Story

SAY: Listen carefully as I tell the Bible story. Every time I say the name "Moses" stand up tall and then sit back down.

Baby Moses grew and grew.

He became a little boy, then a bigger boy, then a teenager, and then a man.

When Moses became a man God called him to lead the Hebrew people out of Egypt, away from the mean Pharaoh.

Moses did what God wanted him to do. He led the people out of Egypt into the desert.

Moses was an important leader.

Once the people were safe in the desert Moses continued to lead the people.

Every day many, many people would line up to see him. They wanted Moses to help them with all their problems.

Moses helped each person. It took ALL day.

At the end of the day, he was very tired.

But the next day, the people would line up again and Moses would spend the day helping each one.

One day a man named Jethro came to Moses. Jethro was Moses' father-in-law.

"Moses," said Jethro, "you are working too hard. Soon you will be so tired you can't do anything. You need to find other people to work together with you."

Moses thought that Jethro had a good idea. So he chose some people who loved God to be leaders.

These leaders worked together to help all the people who came to see Moses.

The people working together made being an important leader much easier for Moses.

Respond to the Bible Story

Response Prayer

SAY: **Repeat after me.**

God, we know we can't do it on our own.

Help us be leaders who ask for help.

Amen.

Response Activity

Show the Bible Story Poster again.

ASK: **How do you think Moses felt when so many people wanted him to help them? How do you think Moses felt when he had other leaders to work together with him?**

SAY: **Heroes are called to work together.**

Have the children stand in a circle. Sing the song, "Heroes Are Called" to the tune of "Here We Go Round the Mulberry Bush." Encourage them to march around the circle as they sing.

Heroes are called to work together, work together, work together.
Heroes are called to work together.
And I'm going to be a hero!
(*Stop marching. Point to self.*)

Split the children into pairs. Encourage children to hold hands and sing the song "Heroes are Called" again as they move around in a circle.

Repeat again, and join more groups together until you have your entire group in one big circle.

SAY: **We are all better when we work together!**

Hotline Verse

Open the Bible.

SAY: **Our Bible verse is "So let's strive for the things that bring peace and the things that build each other up."**

*Teach the children American Sign Language for the words **peace** and **build**.*

Lead the children in saying the verse again and signing the words.

Bible Story
Jethro Mentors Moses
Exodus 18

Hotline Verse
So let's strive for the things that bring peace and the things that build each other up.
(Romans 14:19)

Hotline Tip
Heroes are called to...
Work Together!

Leader Tip
- Reference the Hero Hotline Sign Language document for all ASL signs.

Bible Story

Jethro Mentors Moses
Exodus 18

Hotline Verse

So let's strive for the things that bring peace and the things that build each other up. (Romans 14:19)

Hotline Tip

Heroes are called to... Work Together!

Preschool Recreation

Work Together

Preparation

Make sure the recreation area is safe and ready for play.

Let's Play!

Say: **Heroes are called to work together. Let's work together to play a game.**

1. Have the Heroes stand on one side of the room.

2. Give instructions such as the following:

Hero (*child's name*) **hold Hero** (*child's name*) **hand and skip together across the room.**

Hero (*child's name*) **hold Hero** (*child's name*) **hand and gallop together across the room.**

Hero (*child's name*) **hold Hero** (*child's name*) **hand and hop together around the table one time.**

Hero (*child's name*) **hold Hero** (*child's name*) **hand and sit down together on the same chair.**

Hero (*child's name*) **hold Hero** (*child's name*) **hand and tiptoe together across the room.**

Hero (*child's name*) **hold Hero** (*child's name*) **hand and walk backward together across the room.**

Bible Tie-in

When you are finished, congratulate the children on being such good Heroes.

SAY: **Heroes are called to work together!**

Moses Tag

Preparation

Make sure the recreation area is safe and ready for play.

Let's Play!

SAY: **Moses chose other people to be leaders.**

1. Have the children move to an open area of the room.

2. Choose one child to be Moses.

3. Have the rest of the children walk around the room. Have Moses try to tag a child. When a child is tagged, have the child hold hands with Moses. The tagged child has become one Moses' leaders. Now Moses and the leader work together to try to tag another child and make a group of three.

4. After there is a group of three choose a different Moses and play the game again.

Tip: Help the children play the game once so that they understand the rules. Play the game until each child has an opportunity to be Moses.

Bible Tie-in

SAY: **Moses chose other people to work together with him to lead the people.**

SAY: **Heroes are called to work together.**

Cokesbury Craft
Phone Booth Prayer Box

Purpose
To make a prayer box in which Heroes can put prayers.

Ages
Appropriate for all ages. Young Heroes may need assistance.

Preparation
• Cover the tables with tablecloths.
• Set out supplies.
• Make sure Heroes write their names on their crafts.

Directions
Step 1: Have the children color the phone booth images on all sides of the prayer box.

Step 2: To close the bottom: Fold down the edge with two wings. Fold in the sides and slip the side flaps under the top edge. Insert the bottom edge into the created slot.

Step 3: To close the top: Fold in the three side flaps and insert them into the top. Tape in place if desired.

Step 4: Cut apart the prayer cards. Help children write or draw prayers on the prayer cards and place them in the prayer box.

Bible Tie-in
SAY: **Heroes in old hero cartoons would call for help or change into their hero costume in a phone booth. As God's Heroes, we call on God for help! We can pray to God and ask God to help us with anything we need.**
• **What do you pray for?**

Bible Story
Jethro Mentors Moses
Exodus 18

Hotline Verse
So let's strive for the things that bring peace and the things that build each other up.
(Romans 14:19)

Hotline Tip
Heroes are called to…
Help Others!

Materials
• **Hero Hotline Tablecloth** or other table covering
• **Phone Booth Prayer Box** (one for each Hero)
• markers or crayons
• clear tape
• scissors (for children)

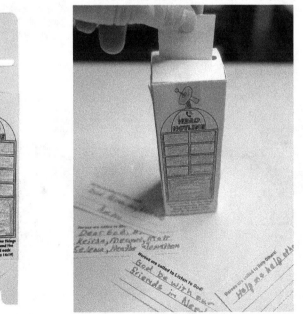

Bible Story
Jethro Mentors Moses
Exodus 18

Hotline Verse
So let's strive for the things that bring peace and the things that build each other up.
(Romans 14:19)

Hotline Tip
Heroes are called to...
Work Together!

Materials
- golf balls
- copy paper
- permanent marker
- scissors
- box lids or plastic tubs
- washable paint
- shallow containers for paint spoons

Make-It-and-Take-It Bible Craft
Work Together Painting

Purpose
Heroes will work together to create art.

Preparation
Fold copy paper in half. Print the Bible verse on each half of the paper. Photocopy the Bible verses paper for each child.

Pour washable paint into shallow containers. Prepare at least two colors of paint. If you have a large group of children, prepare more than one box lid or tub.

Directions
1. Have the children choose a partner.

2. Show the pair how to hold the box lid or tub between them.

3. Place the Bible verses paper inside the box lid or plastic tub.

4. Carefully drop a golf ball into a paint container. Stir the paint to coat the golf ball. Use a spoon to remove the ball and place it on the paper in the lid or tub. Add more golf balls as desired.

5. Encourage the children to work together to move the lid or tub back and forth and up and down to make the golf balls roll across the paper. The balls will leave a trail of paint, making a colorful painting.

6. Set the painting aside to dry. Write both children's names on the painting. When the painting is dry, cut the paper in half so that each child has a painted Bible verse.

SAY: **Heroes are called to work together**.

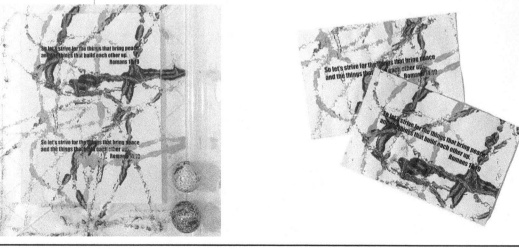

Make-It-and-Take-It Bible Craft
Musical Mural

Purpose
Heroes will work together to create art.

Preparation
Tape a long piece of butcher paper to the top of a table or on the floor. If you are using a table, remove the chairs. Use a permanent marker to write, "Heroes are called to work together," across the mural in big letters. Place markers or crayons around the edge of the paper.

Directions
1. Have the children stand in a circle around the mural paper.

SAY: **We're going to work together to make a colorful mural for our room.**

2. Play the music and encourage them to move around the table or paper.

3. Stop the music and have the children stop moving.

4. Have each child pick a crayon or marker that's lying on the paper near him or her. Encourage the child to use that crayon or marker to draw on the mural.

5. Start the music again. Have them to stop drawing, place the crayons or markers back on the table, and start moving around the table again.

6. Stop the music. Now have each child draw in this new spot. Continue as they show interest.

7. Display the mural in your room.

SAY: **Heroes are called to work together.**

Bible Story
Jethro Mentors Moses
Exodus 18

Hotline Verse
So let's strive for the things that bring peace and the things that build each other up.
(Romans 14:19)

Hotline Tip
Heroes are called to...
Work Together!

Materials
- **Hero Hotline Complete Music CD**
- CD player
- butcher paper
- permanent marker
- crayons or markers
- tape

Bible Story
Jethro Mentors Moses
Exodus 18

Hotline Verse
So let's strive for the things that bring peace and the things that build each other up.
(Romans 14:19)

Hotline Tip
Heroes are called to...
Work Together!

Materials
- flour
- salt
- oil
- water
- red and yellow food coloring
- two mixing bowls
- two mixing spoons
- two sets of measuring cups and spoons
- resealable plastic bags
- permanent marker

Preschool Science
Work Together to Make Orange, Soft Modeling Dough

Preparation:
Write each child's name on a resealable plastic bag.

Directions:
1. Divide the children into two groups. Each group will work together to make either blue or red soft modeling dough. Have the children take turns adding and mixing the ingredients according to the recipe below.

Modeling Dough
- 3 cups flour
- 1 cup salt
- 1 tablespoon oil
- 1 cup water with yellow food coloring OR 1 cup water with red food coloring

2. Help the children mix the flour and salt together in the bowl. Gradually add the water and oil. If the mixture is too stiff, add more water. If the mixture is too sticky, add more flour.

3. For each group: Divide the dough among the children. Encourage the children to knead the dough.

4. Have the children find a partner with the opposite color of dough. If a child has yellow dough, pair with a child who has red dough.

5. Help each child divide their dough in half. Let the partners exchange dough colors. Each child should now have a portion of yellow modeling dough and a portion of red modeling dough.

6. Encourage each child to mix the two colors together and knead the dough.

ASK: **What color have we made?**
(*orange*)

SAY: **In our Bible story, Moses chose a few people to work together to help him lead all the people. We worked together to make orange dough. Heroes are called to work together.**

7. Give children time to play with the dough. Encourage the children to make hero shapes or shapes from the Bible story.

8. Place each piece of orange soft modeling dough in each child's resealable bag.

What's Happening?
The children worked together to make soft modeling dough to share. Then they worked together again to make the red and yellow soft modeling dough orange.

Snack

Work Together to Make Ice Cream

Directions

1. Put all the ingredients in the smaller can.

2. Place the lid on the can and secure it with duct tape.

Tip: If you don't have a lid for the cans, use several layers of plastic wrap. Place the wrap over the top of the can and secure with a large rubber band. Then wrap the top with duct tape.

3. Place the small can inside the larger can. Pour about 6 cups of crushed ice around the smaller can. Add 1 cup of rock salt on the ice.

4. Put the lid on the larger can. Secure the lid with duct tape.

Tip: The smaller can must fit inside the larger can with a little space to add ice. If you have trouble finding aluminum coffee cans, try large vegetable or fruit cans.

5. Spread a plastic tablecloth on the floor. Have the children sit on the edge of the plastic cloth. Encourage the children to roll the can on the floor back and forth to each other over the plastic cloth.

6. Open the large can and take out the small can. Pour off the melted ice and salt mixture.

7. Open the small can and show the children the ice cream. Scrape the ice cream from the sides and stir.

8. Put the lid back on the small can and secure with duct tape. Place the small can back in the larger can.

9. Pour the remaining ice and salt around the small can.

10. Secure the top of the large can again.

11. Roll the can back and forth over the plastic tablecloth for about 10 minutes.

12. Open and serve the ice cream in small bowls or cups.

SAY: **Heroes, you are working together to make today's snack.**

Tip: Prepare the cans and other ingredients ahead of time so that you are ready to move through this activity quickly to keep preschoolers' attention.

Tip: If you have a large group, make more than one can of ice cream. Or purchase cups of ice cream for the children's snack and just give everyone a taste of the homemade ice cream.

Bible Story
Jethro Mentors Moses
Exodus 18

Hotline Verse
So let's strive for the things that bring peace and the things that build each other up.
(Romans 14:19)

Hotline Tip
Heroes are called to... Work Together!

Materials
- modeling dough made earlier
- drinking straws

Bible Story
Jethro Mentors Moses
Exodus 18

Hotline Verse
So let's strive for the things that bring peace and the things that build each other up.
(Romans 14:19)

Hotline Tip
Heroes are called to...
Work Together!

Supplies
• **Scripture Treasure Lanyard** and **Session 3 Stickers**

Leader Tip
Reference the Hero Hotline Sign Language document for all ASL signs.

Reflection Time

Talk About It

ASK: **Who works together in our city?** (*teachers and principals, trash and recycle trucks, police and fire departments*) **In our church?** (*pastors and staff, congregation*) **In your family?** (*parents and children, siblings*)

Prayer

Thank you, God for people who work together. Thank you for (*name each teacher and child*). **Amen.**

Reflection Time Activity

Have the children sit in a circle. Teach the children the word **work** *using the ASL sign.*

Teacher: **Heroes are called...**
Children: **to work together**
All: **I want to be a Hero!**
(*Have the children hold out their arms like they are flying.*)

Go to each child and give a **Session 3 sticker** for their **Scripture Treasure Lanyard.**

SAY: **Hero** (*child's name*) **you are called to work together.**

SAY: **Our Bible verse is "So let's strive for the things that bring peace and the things that build each other up."**

Teach the children American Sign Language for the words **peace, build,** *and* **up.**

Lead the children in saying the verse again and signing the three words.

Bible Beginnings

Hero Hotline Manipulatives

During each session, select one or two of these items as arrival activities for the children to use:

- wood or foam puzzles
- large floor puzzles
- lacing cards
- plastic interlocking blocks
- matching card games/activities

Encourage children to work together to complete these activities. Repeat the theme verse as they play together.

Teamwork Fun
Star Search

- Cover a classroom table with a bed sheet or use a play tent.
- Attach glow-in-the-dark stars to the inside area of the tent.
- Have children use flashlights to discover the stars.
- Ask them to count the stars. Tell them they will be hearing a Bible story about some wise Heroes who listened to God and followed a bright star to find Jesus
- Place storybooks and storybook Bibles in the tent and allow children to spend quiet time reading.

Curiosity Corner
Wonder Sound Box

Before the children arrive, add to the box several items that create sound. Tell them they need to listen to the sound being made in order to guess what it is. A leader will open the lid and play with one of the objects.

SAY: **I wonder what item makes this type of sound. Let's guess! Allow children to guess what the item is.**

Tell the children they will discover a Bible story today about some wise people who listened to God. Repeat the Hotline Tip for this session.

Creation Cavern
Cave Chalk Drawings

- Depending on the size of your sandpaper, you may need to pre-cut sheets.

- Make sure each child's name is on the back of their sandpaper before they start this activity.

Encourage children to create designs similar to ones that would be in a cave. Suggest they blow chalk on their pictures to add fun and interest to this activity.

Optional: Have a larger piece of sandpaper that children can work on together in pairs or small groups.

Bible Story
The Magnificent Magi
Matthew 2:1-12

Hotline Verse
So let's strive for the things that bring peace and the things that build each other up.
(Romans 14:19)

Hotline Tip
Heroes are called to... Listen to God!

Materials
Star Search
- bed sheet or play tent
- glow-in-the-dark stars
- tape
- flashlights

Wonder Sound Box
- small box with lid
- keys
- jingle bells
- silverware
- dry pasta noodles
- rice
- marbles

Cave Chalk Drawings
- superfine sandpaper
- colored chalk
- marker (teacher's use)

Bible Story

The Magnificent Magi
Matthew 2:1-12

Hotline Verse

So let's strive for the things that bring peace and the things that build each other up.
(Romans 14:19)

Hotline Tip

Heroes are called to...
Listen to God!

Gathering Time

Super Meer: **Hello Heroes. Welcome back! Has anyone seen Professor ___ yet today?** (*pauses*) **I haven't either. I've been working on a new superpower and I thought I'd try it out today. I have been working on mind-reading. You know, the power to read someone else's thoughts. Here let me show you. I want all of you to think of your favorite color. Got it? Great!** (*looks to general spot in audience*) **Ok, you right there. You were thinking of the color blue, weren't you?**

Professor: (*arrives late*) **Sorry I'm late. What did I miss?**

Super Meer: **Oh, not too much. I was just showcasing my newest superpower.**

Professor: **Oh, really? What is it?**

Super Meer: **I can read a person's thoughts. In fact, I am reading yours right now and you don't think I can do it, do you?**

Professor: **Well, that is true.**

Super Meer: **Let me prove it to you. Think of a number between 1 and 10.**

Professor: (*ponders a number*) **OK, I got it.**

Super Meer: **I can tell that you are thinking of the number 314.**

Professor: **No, that's not it.**

Super Meer: **Ok, I give up. What was it?**

Professor: **It was two.**

Super Meer: **Two? Of course, it was two. That was my next guess.**

Professor: **Uh-huh. I'm sure it was. What am I thinking now?**

Super Meer: (*strains to think*) **You are thinking that I need to stop reading your mind.**

Professor: **Why yes, I am. And, I'm also thinking we need to get to work.**

Super Meer: **Great idea. Did you bring any snacks?**

Professor: **Snacks? No, I didn't, but we did have an important call earlier from The Pigeon.**

Super Meer: **Wow, a superhero named The Pigeon. Did you know pigeons can fly up to about 75 miles per hour and have amazing hearing? So, what seems to be the trouble with The Pigeon?**

Professor: **Well, I'm not too sure. He had a hard time hearing me.**

Super Meer: **Hmm... Pigeons usually hear really well.**

Professor: **Yes, I know.**

Super Meer: **And I know what you are thinking.**

Professor: **Are you trying to read my mind again?**

Super Meer: **You are thinking we need to look in our Hero Reference Manual. Is that right?**

Professor: **Actually, yes that is correct.** (*pulls out book*) **Let me see here. Well, here is a story that looks like it could help.**

Super Meer: **Does it have any pigeons in it?**

Professor: **I'm not sure. But it does have some wise men who heard a message from God.**

Super Meer: **I hope the story can help with The Pigeon's hearing problem.**

Professor: **Me too. Now I think we...**

Super Meer: (*interrupts*) **Should send these Heroes with our Sidekicks to do some digging into the story?**

Professor: **Why, yes! It's like you took...**

Super Meer: (*interrupts*) **The thoughts right out of your mind?**

Professor: **I was going to say the words right out of my mouth, but very close. Before we send them out, we do need to...**

Super Meer: (*interrupts*) **Go over our Hotline Verse?**

Professor: **Not bad, Super Meer. Yes, let's review our Hotline Verse. It comes from Romans 14:19, "So, let's strive for the things that bring peace and the things that build each other up."** (*Demonstrate hand motions as necessary.*)

Super Meer: **Well done. And here's our Hotline Tip to remember as you go: Heroes are called to listen to God.**

Professor: **Heroes, up, up, and away to learn more!**

Bible Story
The Magnificent Magi
Matthew 2:1-12

Hotline Verse
So let's strive for the things that bring peace and the things that build each other up.
(Romans 14:19)

Hotline Tip
Heroes are called to...
Listen to God!

Bible Story

The Magnificent Magi
Matthew 2:1-12

Hotline Verse

So let's strive for the
things that bring peace
and the things that build
each other up.
(Romans 14:19)

Hotline Tip

Heroes are called to...
Listen to God!

Materials

- **Hero Hotline Complete
  Music CD**
- towels
- various sizes of
  aluminum and stainless
  steel bowls
- stainless steel and
  aluminum pot lids
- plastic, metal, and
  wooden mixing spoons
- container of water

Music and Mission Times

Before You Teach

- Select the number of songs and activities that will best fill in your available
  time.
- Gather the necessary items for the music and rhythm activities.
- Play the Hero Hotline Complete Music CD as the children enter and exit
  Music Time.

Suggested Songs

- "Hero Hotline" (Theme Song)
- "Let's Strive"
- "Show Grace, Speak Truth"

Fun with Music

Before the children listen to sounds
through water play, have them listen
to and sing a couple of their favorite
songs from VBS. Encourage them
to move about as the music is being
played.

Listening to Sounds Through Water Play

1. Cover the area with towels.

2. Encourage children to add
   various amounts of water to the
   containers. Show them how to use
   plastic and metal mixing spoons
   as strikers to tap the containers.

3. Ask them to listen to the various
   sounds that are made as they
   strike the containers. Help them
   describe the sounds they hear.

4. Remind the children of their Bible
   story and the Hotline Tip. Ask
   them to repeat the Hotline Tip.
   Talk about ways Heroes listen to
   God and one another.

Rhythm Activity

Play a game of Freeze to encourage
listening and following directions.

- Children will jump, walk fast, and
  dance as they listen to the Hero
  Hotline music.

- When the music stops, children
  are to freeze in place. Make sure
  all children stop in place before
  starting the activity once more.

- At the end of this activity, ask the
  children to sit on the floor.

SAY: **Heroes are called to listen to
God!**

Stop and have a short prayer before
the children go to the next activity.

Mission Time

Mission Time will feature hands-on
ideas. There are several options.
Look in the Mission Leader book and
select the options that best fit the
needs of your church.

Experience the Bible Story

Transition to the Bible Story

Invite the Heroes to stop their current activity and prepare for the Bible story by joining in this action rhyme:

Who you gonna call?
(*Cup hands around mouth, face front.*)
Who you gonna call?
(*Cup hands around mouth, face to the side.*)
Who you gonna call?
(*Cup hands around mouth, face to the other side.*)
Hero Hotline!
(*Pretend to fly around the room like a superhero.*)
Why?
(*Stop moving. Shrug shoulders.*)
Because Heroes listen to God!
(*Cup your hands around your ears.*)

Who you gonna call?
(*Cup hands around mouth, face front.*)
Who you gonna call?
(*Cup hands around mouth, face to the side.*)
Who you gonna call?
(*Cup hands around mouth, face to the other side.*)
Hero Hotline!
(*Pretend to fly around the room like a superhero. Stop.*)

Get Ready

Show the children the Bible.

SAY: **This is our Bible. It is a special book that tells us about God and the people who followed God. The Bible has two parts.** (*Turn to Genesis.*) **The Old Testament. The Old Testament has stories about many men and women who loved God.** (*Turn to Matthew.*) **The second part of our Bible is** the New Testament. **The New Testament has many stories about Jesus and people who followed Jesus.** (*Turn to Matthew.*) **Today our Bible story is from the New Testament. It's a story about some wise men. In this story Jesus is a young toddler.** (*Place the Bible in your story area.*)

The wise men saw a special star in the sky. They believed that the star meant a new king had been born. They decided to search for this new king. The star led the wise men to Bethlehem and to Jesus. Let's make stars.

Star Signs

• Photocopy and cut out the Star Circle for each child, or purchase foam star cutouts from a craft store.

• Give each child a star circle. Let the children decorate the star with crayons or markers.

• Give each child a paper plate. Have the children glue the star circles or foam star cutouts onto the paper plates.

• Write each child's name on the back of the plate. Help each child tape a craft stick to the back of the star to make a handle.

• Have the children hold up their stars and do a star parade as they follow you to the story area.

Bible Story

The Magnificent Magi
Matthew 2:1-12

Hotline Verse

So let's strive for the things that bring peace and the things that build each other up.
(Romans 14:19)

Hotline Tip

Heroes are called to... Listen to God!

Materials:

• **Session 3 Bible Story Poster** or Bible storybook
• **Star Circle Template** (found in the Free Resources section at www.CokesburyVBS. com)
• foam star cutouts
• scissors
• crayons or markers
• paper plates
• glue sticks
• craft sticks
• tape

Bible Story

The Magnificent Magi
Matthew 2:1-12

Hotline Verse

So let's strive for the things that bring peace and the things that build each other up.
(Romans 14:19)

Hotline Tip

Heroes are called to...
Listen to God!

Materials

- Star Signs made previously

Tell the Bible Story

SAY: Listen carefully as I tell the Bible story. Every time I say the word _star_, hold up your _star_ signs.

"Look at that _star_!" said the first wise man. "It is shining so brightly."

"It is brighter than all the other _stars_," said the second wise man.

"I wonder what the _star_ means," said the third wise man.

"It must mean a new king is born," said the first wise man.

"Let's follow the _star_ to find the new king," said the second wise man.

So the wise men loaded their camels with food and water for a long journey. They also packed special gifts for the new king.

The wise men started on their journey. They traveled by night, following the _star_.

The _star_ led them to King Herod's palace. But the new king was not there, only the mean King Herod.

"Where is the newborn king?" asked the first wise man.

"We have been following his _star_," said the second wise man.

King Herod was upset. He did not want a new king to be born. He wanted to stay the only king. But he asked his helpers to find out where this new king was to be born.

"A new king is to be born in

Bethlehem," said King Herod's helpers.

"Go to Bethlehem," said King Herod. "When you find the new king, come back and tell me so that I may also go and take him gifts."

But what King Herod really wanted was to find this new king and get rid of him!

The wise men left King Herod and followed the _star_ to a little town called Bethlehem.

"Look, the _star_ has stopped!" said the first wise man.

"The _star_ is shining right over the house," said the second wise man.

"The new king must be inside," said the third wise man.

So the wise men unpacked their gifts and went inside the house. They saw Jesus and his mother, Mary. Jesus was the new king!

The wise men knelt beside Jesus and gave him gifts of gold, frankincense, and myrrh.

That night the wise men had a dream. The dream told them to go home a different way instead of going to see King Herod.

The wise men knew that the dream was from God. They listened to God and went home another way. As they went home, the wise men were happy they had followed the _star_ and found Jesus.

Respond to the Bible Story

Response Prayer

SAY: **Repeat after me.**

God you have given us helping hands
(*hands palms up*)
And listening ears
(*cup hands around ears*)
And feet to follow (*walk in place*)
Help us be a hero for you, God
(*hands on hips in superhero pose*)!
Amen.

Response Activity

Show the Bible Story Poster again.

ASK: **The wise men listened to God. How can we listen to God?**
(*pray, hear Bible stories, come to church, listen as our parents and teachers tell us about God.*)

SAY: **Heroes are called to listen to God.**

- Have the children stand in a circle. Sing the song, "Heroes Are Called" to the tune of "Here We Go Round the Mulberry Bush." Encourage the children to march around the circle as they sing.

Heroes are called to listen to God, listen to God, listen to God.
Heroes are called to listen to God. And I'm going to be a hero!
(*Stop marching. Point to self.*)

SAY: **Let's follow the star just like the wise men in the story.**

- Choose one child to be the Leader. Give that child their star sign and have the other children line up behind the leader.
- Walk or march around the room as you sing "Heroes Are Called."
- Repeat as necessary and give other children a chance to be the leader. Encourage children to do different motions or actions each time.

Hotline Verse

Open the Bible.

SAY: **Our Bible verse is "So let's strive for the things that bring peace and the things that build each other up."**

*Teach the children American Sign Language for the words **peace** and **build**.*

Lead the children in saying the verse again and signing the words.

Bible Story
The Magnificent Magi
Matthew 2:1-12

Hotline Verse
So let's strive for the things that bring peace and the things that build each other up.
(Romans 14:19)

Hotline Tip
Heroes are called to... Listen to God!

Leader Tip
Reference the Hero Hotline Sign Language document for all ASL signs.

Bible Story
The Magnificent Magi
Matthew 2:1-12

Hotline Verse
So let's strive for the things that bring peace and the things that build each other up.
(Romans 14:19)

Hotline Tip
Heroes are called to...
Listen to God!

Materials
Walk Like a Camel
• one of the star signs made earlier

Preschool Recreation

Listen!

Preparation
Make sure the recreation area is safe and ready for play.

Let's Play!
SAY: **Heroes are called to listen to God. Let's play a game like Simon Says. We'll call it Hero Says. When you hear me say "Hero Says," do whatever motion I tell you to do. But listen carefully. If I do not say "Hero Says," do not do the motion.**

1. Play this game like "Simon Says." You or another Sidekick will be the Hero.

2. Have the children line up facing the Hero.

3. The Hero calls out a number and motions by first saying, "Hero says..." (hop, jump, run in place, etc.) The children must perform that motion.

4. Anytime the Hero calls out a motion without saying, "Hero says..." the children should NOT do it. If anyone does, do not make them stop the game. Just say, "Uh oh! I did not say Hero Says." And then continue with all the children.

Bible Tie-in
SAY: **The wise men listened to God. Heroes are called to listen to God.**

Walk Like a Camel

Preparation
Make sure the recreation area is safe and ready for play.

Let's Play!
SAY: Sometimes we see pictures of the wise men riding camels. Let's pretend to be camels.

1. Show the children how to bend slightly at the waist and to do a bumpy/jerky kind of walk similar to how a camel would do in the sand.

2. Have the children practice camel walking.

3. Explain that the children are all part of a camel caravan, a group of camels crossing the desert. Everyone must follow single file.

4. Hold up the star sign and let the children pretend to be camels as they follow you all around the room and out into the hall.

Bible Tie-in
SAY: **In our Bible story, the wise men followed a bright star to find the new king.**

Cokesbury Craft
Hero Signal Suncatcher

Purpose
To make a reminder of our time at VBS.

Ages
Appropriate for all ages.

Preparation
• Cover tables with tablecloths.
• Set out all supplies.
• Place a suncatcher on a paper plate for each Hero. Write the Hero's name on the paper plate.

Directions
Step 1: Color in the spaces on the Hero Signal Suncatcher with markers or glitter paint.

Tips: If you're comfortable letting the children use them, permanent markers work best. You may also try glitter glue pens or acrylic paint with this craft. Be sure to provide smocks, cover surfaces, and use non-toxic supplies when possible. Be sure to supervise preschoolers when using supplies like permanent markers or paint.

Step 2: Set the suncatchers aside to dry.

Step 3: Hang the suncatcher in a window in your room or home to remind you of your time at VBS.

Bible Tie-in
SAY: **The light that shone from the star led the magi on their journey. When light shines through your suncatcher, you can be reminded that you are God's hero, and that you are part of a team working for God in the world.**
• Who is on your hero team? Who in your life helps you follow God?

Bible Story
The Magnificent Magi
Matthew 2:1-12

Hotline Verse
So let's strive for the things that bring peace and the things that build each other up.
(Romans 14:19)

Hotline Tip
Heroes are called to...
Listen to God!

Materials
• **Hero Central Tablecloth** or other table covering
• **Hero Signal Suncatchers**
• markers or glitter paint and paintbrushes (permanent markers work best)
• paper plates
• pens or pencils

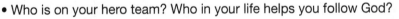

Bible Story
The Magnificent Magi
Matthew 2:1-12

Hotline Verse
So let's strive for the things that bring peace and the things that build each other up.
(Romans 14:19)

Hotline Tip
Heroes are called to...
Listen to God!

Materials
• **Hero Hotline Tablecloths** or other table coverings
• Star Circle Template (found in the Free Resources section www.CokesburyVBS.com)
• drinking straws
• washable paint
• spoon
• smocks

Make-It-and-Take-It Bible Craft
Stars and Straws

Purpose
Heroes will make a painting as a reminder of the Bible story.

Preparation
Photocopy the star circle for each child.

Cover tables with Hero Hotline tablecloths or paper.

Directions
1. Have the children wear smocks.

2. Give each child a copy of the star circle and a straw.

3. Show the children how to blow through the straw. Remind the children that they are blowing into the straw, not sucking. Have the children blow through the straw so that they feel the air on one of their hands.

SAY: **Heroes, you are good listeners! Heroes are called to listen to God.**

4. Spoon a small amount of paint in the center of each child's star.

5. Encourage the children to blow the paint with the straws so that the paint spreads around their stars.

SAY: **Our Bible story is about the wise men who saw a bright star in the sky. They thought that the star meant a special king had been born. They followed the star to find the new king. The star led the wise men to Bethlehem and Jesus.**

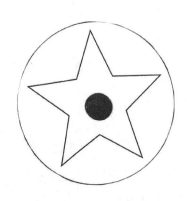

Make-It-and-Take-It Craft
Star Ornaments

Purpose
Heroes will create a reminder of the Bible story.

Preparation
Using a hot glue gun, glue 5 small craft sticks in the shape of a star for each child. If you have more time, this may also be done with regular glue.

Cut yarn into 24-to-36" pieces. You will need at least 3 or 4 pieces per child.

Also cut yarn into 8" pieces, one per child.

Tip: Make your stars ahead of time and allow plenty of time to dry before doing this craft.

Directions
Option 1:
1. Give each child a star.

2. Tie one piece of yarn to each child's star.

3. Show children how to wrap the yarn around the edges of the star.

4. When you near the end of one piece of yarn, attach a new piece either by tying a knot or by placing the end of the new piece behind the star and wrapping the first piece around it. You may choose to cut an extra-long piece of yarn.

5. When each child is finished, help them tuck in the ends of the yarn or secure the ends with a small dot of glue.

6. Attach a smaller piece of yarn with hot glue to turn the star into an ornament.

Bible Story
The Magnificent Magi
Matthew 2:1-12

Hotline Verse
So let's strive for the things that bring peace and the things that build each other up.
(Romans 14:19)

Hotline Tip
Heroes are called to...
Listen to God!

Materials
- **Hero Hotline Tablecloths** or other table coverings
- **Hero Hotline Craft Theme Stickers**
- craft sticks
- hot glue gun (adult use only)
- glue
- yarn (various colors)
- stick-on gems or pom poms

Leader Tip:
If you do not wish to make stars out of craft sticks, you may choose to trace and cut stars out of sturdy cardboard. Use the the Star Template found in the Free Resources section at www.CokesburyVBS.com to make a star for each child.

Option 2:

1. Give each child a star.

2. Encourage children to decorate their star with stickers, stick-on gems, or pom poms.

Bible Story
The Magnificent Magi
Matthew 2:1-12

Hotline Verse
So let's strive for the things that bring peace and the things that build each other up.
(Romans 14:19)

Hotline Tip
Heroes are called to...
Listen to God!

Materials:
• bowl
• plastic wrap
• large rubber band
• sprinkles

Preschool Science
Good Vibrations

Preparation:

1. Tear plastic wrap to cover the top of the bowl. Secure the plastic wrap around the bowl with a large rubber band. Pull on the edges of the plastic wrap to make the wrap taut across the top of the bowl.

2. Shake sprinkles onto the plastic wrap.

Directions:
Let the children take turns placing their lips close to the edge of the bowl (not touching) and humming. The sprinkles will dance!

Tip: Have wipes handy to wipe the bowl after each child to prevent spreading germs, or have one bowl per child if possible.

What's Happening?
Sound vibrations are causing the plastic wrap to move, making the sprinkles dance.

SAY: **God gave us our ears to hear. Heroes are called to listen to God!**

Preschool Science
Cup-and-String Telephones

Preparation:

Use a sharp pencil to punch a hole in the bottom of each cup. Cut yarn or string into lengths at least 24" long. Wrap a piece of tape around each end.

Tip: You will need two cups, two paper clips, and one length of string for each Cup-and-String Telephone set.

Directions

1. Give each child two paper cups. Let the children decorate the outside of the cups with stickers.

2. Give each child a length of yarn or string. Show the child how to thread the taped end through the hole of one cup from the outside to the inside. Tie the end of the yarn or string inside the cup to a paper clip. Repeat with the second cup.

3. Help the children pull on the cups to tighten the yarn or string.

4. Have the children find a partner and choose one set of cups to begin the experiment. Each child should take a cup. The first child holds the cup up to her or his ear. The second child holds the cup up to his or her mouth. Have the children move apart until the string is stretched taut.

5. Encourage the children to hold the cups close to their mouths to whisper into the cups. Ask the children holding the cups to their ears if they can hear what is being said.

6. Encourage the children to take turns talking and listening.

7. Have the children try the second set of cups.

SAY: **In our Bible story, the wise men listened to a message from God. The message came in their dreams, not on a telephone.**

ASK: **How can we listen to God?** (*praying, hearing Bible stories, coming to church or VBS, paying attention as teachers and parents talk about God*)

SAY: **Heroes are called to listen to God!**

What's Happening?

When you speak into the cup, your voice makes sound vibrations or movements. We can't see the vibrations, but they move into the string. Then the vibrations travel through the string, as long as it is held taut, into the cup. The vibrations go into the air in the cup, around the listener's ear, allowing the whisper to be heard even when standing far apart.

Bible Story

The Magnificent Magi
Matthew 2:1-12

Hotline Verse

So let's strive for the things that bring peace and the things that build each other up. (Romans 14:19)

Hotline Tip

Heroes are called to... Listen to God!

Materials:

- **Hero Hotline Craft Theme Stickers**
- plastic or paper cups
- string or yarn
- tape
- paper clips
- sharp pencil

Bible Story
The Magnificent Magi
Matthew 2:1-12

Hotline Verse
So let's strive for the
things that bring peace
and the things that build
each other up.
(Romans 14:19)

Hotline Tip
Heroes are called to...
Listen to God!

Ingredients
- 3 cups shaped cereal
  such as Cheerios® or
  Lucky Charms®
- 3 cups wheat or rice
  cereal squares, such as
  Wheat Chex® or Rice
  Chex®
- 1½ cups small pretzels
- 1½ cups raisins or dried
  cranberries

Supplies
- 4 bowls or plastic food
  containers, small cups
- 4 ¼-cup measuring
  cups for scooping
- hand-washing supplies

Snacks
Snacks for the Journey
Directions

1. Place the ingredients in separate
   bowls or plastic food containers.
   Place a ¼ cup measuring spoon
   with each container.

2. Have the children take turns
   scooping ingredients from each
   bowl into their cups.

SAY: **In our Bible story the wise
men made a long journey to find
Jesus. They had to take food on
their journey. Let's make a trail mix
to eat and then go on a journey.**

3. After each child has made the
   snack, have the children line up
   behind you. Take the children on
   a journey around your room and
   then back to the snack table. Or
   take your children on a journey
   outside and enjoy eating your
   snack under the shade of a tree.

4. Say a thank-you prayer. And enjoy
   the snack.

Yield: About 20 servings.

Reflection Time

Talk About It

ASK: **Who or what do you want to listen for?** (*God, the ocean, mom or dad, music, rain, thunder, teachers*)

Prayer

Help us, God, to listen to you. Thank you for (*name each teacher and child*). **Amen.**

Reflection Time Activity

Have the children sit in a circle.

Teacher: **Heroes are called...**
Children: **to listen to God.**
 (*Cup hands around ears.*)
All: **I want to be a hero!**
 (*Have the children hold out their arms like they are flying.*)

Go to each child and give her/ him the **Session 4 sticker** for their **Scripture Treasure Lanyard**.

SAY: **Hero** (*child's name*) **you are called to listen to God.**

SAY: **Our Bible verse is "So let's strive for the things that bring peace and the things that build each other up."**

Teach the children American Sign Language for the words *peace,* and *build.* and *up.*

Lead them in saying the verse again and signing the three words.

Bible Story

The Magnificent Magi
Matthew 2:1-12

Hotline Verse

So let's strive for the things that bring peace and the things that build each other up.
(Romans 14:19)

Hotline Tip

Heroes are called to...
Listen to God!

Materials

- **Scripture Treasure Lanyards** and **Session 4 Stickers**

Bible Story

Unexpected Heroes Give
Paul a Basket Ride
Acts 9:1-25

Hotline Verse

So let's strive for the
things that bring peace
and the things that build
each other up.
(Romans 14:19)

Hotline Tip

Heroes are called to...
Show Grace!

Materials
Beanbag Balance

beanbags

Rock Exploration

- small rocks of various
  sizes and colors
- magnifying glass
- scale
- plastic containers
- picture of the inside of a
  colorful cave

Grace Flowers

- artificial flowers and/or
  greenery
- small plastic vases

Bible Beginnings
Hero Hotline Manipulatives

During each session, select one or two of these items as arrival activities for the
children to use:

- wood or foam puzzles
- large floor puzzles
- lacing cards
- plastic interlocking blocks
- matching card games/activities

Encourage children to work together to complete these activities. Repeat the
theme verse as the children play together.

Teamwork Fun
Beanbag Balance

For this activity, children are to carry
their beanbags on their heads. Give
each child a beanbag to balance on
their head as everyone walks around
the area. If the beanbag falls, the
child must stop and can only move
again if another child performs a
helpful act and picks up the beanbag
for another child.

Curiosity Corner
Rock Exploration

Remind children that inside a cave
there are many sizes and colors
of rock formations. Show children
a picture to help them better
understand this activity. Invite
children to explore the various
rocks. Encourage them to use the
magnifying glass to examine the
rocks. Talk about the textures and
colors of the rocks. Weigh the rocks.
Repeat the theme verse as a group.

Creation Cavern
Grace Flowers

Children will arrange flowers in
vases to share with others. Allow
children time to make a flower gift for
someone. As children as arranging
their flowers talk about how they are
being kind and showing grace.

If you do not have artificial flowers,
have children draw pictures of
flowers on paper.

SAY: **Heroes are called to show
grace to others. Grace is a way
to show God's love to others.
Sometimes, a flower can be a
reminder of grace!**

If possible, invite a staff member
to visit the class and accept the
flower arrangements to help children
understand the act of sharing and
showing grace to others, and how it
feels to give.

Gathering Time

Professor: **Welcome Heroes! I'm so glad you are here today at Hero Hotline Headquarters. I'm sure you've already heard, but there is something strange going on out there. We have been really busy already today.**

Super Meer: (*pops up*) **Speaking of strange, we are officially out of donuts.** (*realizes that audience is present*) **Oops, I didn't know our Heroes were here already.**

Professor: **I sent Super Meer to get a snack. He has been working hard answering these phone calls today. How many has it been already?**

Super Meer: **Phew! About 12 or 13.**

Professor: **That's right. All of the calls have been about...**

Super Meer: **the Smellcaster!**

Professor: (*to audience*) **I know some of you are new recruits and may not have heard about The Smellcaster, but he is someone you definitely want to avoid.**

Super Meer: **Right! He can make things smell really bad.**

Professor: **The problem is that The Smellcaster is telling everyone that he has changed, that he is no longer a bad guy. He is trying to work with the Heroes and make things smell good.**

Super Meer:sProfessor: **I don't blame them. We have an emergency on our hands. We need to find a solution for all of these Heroes in need.**

Super Meer: **I agree. Let's see if we can remember our Hotline Verse.** (*to audience*) **Do you remember where it can be found?** (*pause*) **It's from Romans 14:19. Those of you with super memory powers, say it with me. "So, let's strive for the things that bring peace and the things that build each other up."**

Professor: **We really need to find something that could bring peace and encourage the hero community.**

Super Meer: **Perhaps it is time to refer to our Hero Reference Manual.**

Professor: **Great idea! I have it right here.** (*pulls out book*) **Hmm, what do I look for?**

Super Meer: **This may be a long-shot, but is there anything about a bad guy turning into a good guy?**

Super Meer: **Let me see...** (*looking*) **Well... actually, there is! Let's look at this story. It's about a man named Paul. At first he was really mean to anyone who followed Jesus. But then something surprising happened and he made a big change! He became a follower of Jesus himself. Early Christians were very afraid of him and didn't trust him at first. Does that sound familiar?**

Bible Story
Unexpected Heroes Give Paul a Basket Ride
Acts 9:1-25

Hotline Verse
So let's strive for the things that bring peace and the things that build each other up.
(Romans 14:19)

Hotline Tip
Heroes are called to...
Show Grace!

Bible Story
Unexpected Heroes Give
Paul a Basket Ride
Acts 9:1-25

Hotline Verse
So let's strive for the
things that bring peace
and the things that build
each other up.
(Romans 14:19)

Hotline Tip
Heroes are called to...
Show Grace!

Super Meer: **It sure does. OK,
it looks like our best course of
action is to see if we can learn
more about how all these people
handled Paul's change.**

Professor: **Alright, Heroes. It's time
to head off with our Sidekicks to
learn more about this story.**

Super Meer: **And here's one more
hotline tip to remember as you go:
Heroes are called to show grace!**

Professor: **Heroes, up, up, and
away to learn more!**

Music and Mission Times

Before You Teach

Select the number of songs and activities that will best fill in your available time.

Gather the necessary items for the music and rhythm activities.

Play the Hero Hotline Complete Music CD as the children enter and exit Music Time.

Suggested Songs

- "Hero Hotline" (Theme Song)
- "Show Grace, Speak Truth"

Fun with Music
Bell Bracelets

1. Assist children as they add bells to their chenille stems.

2. Show them how to attach the bracelet together. Add a piece of masking tape around the ends of the stems.

3. Write the name of the child on a piece of masking tape. Add it to their bracelets.

4. Play several songs from the Hero Hotline Complete Music CD.

5. Encourage children to use their bell bracelets as the music is being played.

Rhythm Activity
Show Grace

- Use the Bell Bracelets children made for this activity.

- Have a leader name some actions that illustrate kind and unkind deeds.

- If the action is kind and full of grace have them ring the bell bracelets way up high. If the action is unkind, ask them to ring the bell bracelets way down low.

Remind them of the theme verse. Ask them to repeat it. Talk about ways the kind deeds are ways to bring peace to others.

Here are some options to get you started.

- A friend at the park wanted to play with the wagon first, so I said he could use it first.

- My sister took one of my toys and did not ask me first. I found out later my toy was broken.

- My friend could not ride her tricycle well and I laughed at her.

- I dropped my plate and my brother stopped and helped me clean up the mess.

- I dropped my bottle of bubbles. My friend shared his bottle with me.

Mission Time

Mission Time will feature hands-on ideas. There are several options. Look in the Mission Leader book and select the options that best fit the needs of your church.

Bible Story

Unexpected Heroes Give Paul a Basket Ride
Acts 9:1-25

Hotline Verse

So let's strive for the things that bring peace and the things that build each other up.
(Romans 14:19)

Hotline Tip

Heroes are called to... Show Grace!

Materials
Bell Bracelets

- **Hero Hotline Complete Music CD**
- chenille stems (one per child)
- jingle bells (5-6 per child)
- masking tape
- marker (adult use)

Bible Story

Unexpected Heroes Give
Paul a Basket Ride
Acts 9:1-25

Hotline Verse

So let's strive for the
things that bring peace
and the things that build
each other up.
(Romans 14:19)

Hotline Tip

Heroes are called to...
Show Grace!

Leader Tip

Find and mark Acts in
your Bible ahead of time.

Materials

**Session 5 Bible Story
Poster** or Bible storybook

Experience the Bible Story

Transition to the Bible Story

Invite the Heroes to stop their current
activity and prepare for the Bible
story by joining in this action rhyme.

Who you gonna call?
(*Cup hands around mouth, face
front.*)
Who you gonna call?
(*Cup hands around mouth, face to
the side.*)
Who you gonna call?
(*Cup hands around mouth, face to
the other side.*)
Hero Hotline!
(*Pretend to fly around the room like
a superhero.*)
Why?
(*Stop moving. Shrug shoulders.*)
**Because Heroes are called to
show grace!**
(*Cup your hands around your ears.*)

Who you gonna call?
(*Cup hands around mouth, face
front.*)
Who you gonna call?
(*Cup hands around mouth, face to
the side.*)
Who you gonna call?
(*Cup hands around mouth, face to
the other side.*)
Hero Hotline!
(*Pretend to fly around the room like
a superhero. Stop.*)

Get Ready

Show the children the Bible.

SAY: **This is our Bible. It is a
special book that tells us about
God and the people who followed
God. The Bible has two parts.** (*Turn
to Genesis.*) **The Old Testament.
The Old Testament has stories
about many men and women
who loved God.** (*Turn to Matthew.*)

**The second part of our Bible is
the New Testament. The New
Testament has many stories about
Jesus and people who followed
Jesus. Today our Bible story is
from the New Testament.** (*Turn to
Acts.*) **Today our Bible story is from
the New Testament. It's a story
about a man named Paul. Let's
make a puppet of Paul.**

Paul Puppets

Supplies: large craft sticks or tongue
depressors, crayons or markers,
fabric scraps, glue.

Give each child a stick or tongue
depressor. Show the children how
to make two eyes and a mouth on
one end of the sticks. This will make
Paul's face. Let them choose a scrap
of fabric. Help them glue the fabric
around the stick under Paul's face.

Imagine the Bible Story

Have the Heroes sit. Place the poster
for Session 5 or the storybook Bible
at child's eye level. If you chose to
make the Super Vision Binoculars,
give each child his or her binocular.

SAY: **Let's use our superhero vision
to look at today's story poster!
Look carefully, Heroes. What do
you see?**

Invite the children look through
the binoculars or place their hands
around their eyes (like binoculars).
Encourage them to use their "hero
vision" to look at the Bible story.

SAY: **I wonder what's happening in
this picture? What do you think the
people are doing?**

Tell the Bible Story

SAY: Today's Bible story is about a man named Paul. We will use our puppets as I tell the story. Every time I say the word "Paul," hold up your puppet.

"Followers of Jesus need to be stopped!" said Paul. "They should be put in jail."

Paul and his friends were on their way to a city called Damascus. Paul had heard that there were many followers in Damascus. Paul was going to arrest Jesus' followers and put them in jail.

Suddenly, a bright light from heaven flashed around Paul! He fell to the ground and covered his eyes.

"Paul, Paul," said a voice from the light. "Why are you unkind to my followers?"

It was Jesus' voice!

"Get up, Paul, and go into the city," said Jesus. "Someone will come to help you."

When Paul stood up, he couldn't see! Paul's friends had to lead him.

A man named Ananias lived in the city. He was a follower of Jesus. One day Ananias heard the voice of Jesus.

"Find the man named Paul," said Jesus.

"But Paul is unkind to your followers, Jesus," said Ananias. "I am afraid."

"I have chosen Paul to tell others about me," said Jesus. "You must go to him."

So even though he was afraid, Ananias went to find Paul. Paul was just sitting in a house. He still could not see.

"Paul," said Ananias. "Jesus sent me to help you." Then Ananias touched Paul's face. Immediately, Paul was able to see!

Paul was baptized and became a follower of Jesus. Paul had changed. He began to tell everyone about Jesus.

But some people did not believe Paul had really changed. They thought Paul was trying to trick them.

"Aren't you the same Paul who wanted to put all Jesus' followers in jail?" Asked the people who did not trust Paul.

Some of the people got so mad at Paul; they wanted to hurt him. They planned to catch Paul when he left the city. A tall wall went all the way around the city. The only way out of the city was through the gate. They had guards watching the city gates day and night.

It was time for Paul to go back home, but the way was not a safe. Some of Paul's friends had an idea. They put Paul in a large basket and tied a rope to it. Then they lowered him slowly down from a window in the city wall.

Bible Story
Unexpected Heroes Give Paul a Basket Ride
Acts 9:1-25

Hotline Verse
So let's strive together for the things that bring peace and the things that build each other up. (Romans 14:19)

Hotline Tip
Heroes are called to... Show Grace!

Materials
• Paul puppets made previously

Bible Story

Unexpected Heroes Give
Paul a Basket Ride
Acts 9:1-25

Hotline Verse

So let's strive for the
things that bring peace
and the things that build
each other up.
(Romans 14:19)

Hotline Tip

Heroes are called to...
Show Grace!

Paul made it safely out of the city
with the help of his friends.

Show the Bible Story Poster again.

SAY: **When Paul's friends helped
him, they were showing grace;
that means forgiving someone if
they have done something wrong
and showing love to them. Heroes
are called to show grace.**

Have the children stand in a circle
and sing, "Heroes Are Called."

**Heroes are called to show God's
grace,
show God's grace, show God's
grace.
Heroes are called to show God's
grace.
And I'm going to be a hero!**
(*Stop marching. Point to self.*)

Respond to the Bible Story

Response Prayer

SAY: Repeat after me.
Thank you for your grace, God
Thank you for your grace.
Every day and every way,
Thank you for your grace.
Amen.

Response Activity

SAY: When Paul's friends helped him, they were showing grace. Showing grace means forgiving someone if they have done something wrong and showing them love. Heroes are called to show grace.

Have the children stand in a circle. Sing the song, "Heroes Are Called" to the tune of "Here We Go Round the Mulberry Bush." Encourage the children to march around the circle as they sing.

Heroes are called to show God's grace,
show God's grace, show God's grace.
Heroes are called to show God's grace.
And I'm going to be a hero!
(Stop marching. Point to self.)

Hotline Verse

Open the Bible.

SAY: Our Bible verse is "So let's strive for the things that bring peace and the things that build each other up."

Teach the children American Sign Language for the words peace and build.

Lead the children in saying the verse again and signing the words.

Bible Story
Unexpected Heroes Give Paul a Basket Ride
Acts 9:1-25

Hotline Verse
So let's strive for the things that bring peace and the things that build each other up.
(Romans 14:19)

Hotline Tip
Heroes are called to...
Show Grace!

Bible Story
Unexpected Heroes Give Paul a Basket Ride
Acts 9:1-25

Hotline Verse
So let's strive for the things that bring peace and the things that build each other up.
(Romans 14:19)

Hotline Tip
Heroes are called to... Show Grace!

Materials:
Hide Paul in the Basket
• Paul puppets made earlier
• 2 baskets
• masking tape

A Tisket, A Tasket
• basket
• one Paul puppet made earlier

Preschool Recreation

Hide Paul in the Basket

Preparation
Make sure the recreation area is safe and ready for play. Mark a starting line on the floor with masking tape. Place a basket across the room from the starting line for each team.

Let's Play!
1. Have the children bring their Paul puppets.

2. Divide the children into two teams. Have them line up behind the starting line.

SAY: **Heroes, in our Bible story today, Paul's friends help him by hiding him in a basket and then lowering him over the city's wall. Let's pretend that we are Paul's friends. We want to help him hide in a basket. When I call your name, tiptoe to basket, place your Paul puppet inside the basket, and then run back to your line. Then I will call the name of the next hero in line.**

3. Call the names of the children who are first in line for each team. Remind them to tiptoe to the basket. After they place the Paul figure in the basket, remind them to run back to the line.

4. Continue until all have a turn.

Bible Tie-in
SAY: **Paul's friends helped him by lowering him in a basket over the city wall. Paul's friends showed Paul grace.**

A Tisket, A Tasket

Preparation
Make sure the recreation area is safe and ready for play.

Let's Play!
1. Have the children stand in a circle with their backs to the inside of the circle.

2. Place the Paul puppet in the basket.

SAY: **In our Bible story today, Paul hides in a basket in order to get safely out of the city.**

3. Begin the game yourself. Skip (or walk) around the outside of the circle holding the basket.

SAY: **A tisket, a tasket, hide Paul in the basket.**

4. Stop by one child and place the basket on the floor in front of the child. Have the child pick up the basket and chase you around the circle back to his/her spot.

5. You stand in the child's spot and the child starts the game over again.

Bible Tie-in
SAY: **In our Bible story today, Paul's friends saw and believed that Jesus could change even a heart like Paul's. They saw that Paul now loved Jesus and helped Paul escape to do more of Jesus' work. Paul's friends showed Paul grace.**

SAY: **Heroes are called to show grace.**

Make-It-and-Take-It Craft
Hero Team Frame

Purpose
To create a fun and functional reminder of your time together in VBS.

Ages
Appropriate for all ages. Young Heroes may need assistance.

Preparation
• Cover tables with tablecloths.
• Pre-cut cardboard for frames to approximately 5 ½" x 8 ½".
• Copy the triangle template and cloud template onto thick card stock or cardboard. Cut out a few templates for the Heroes to use.
• Pre-cut six green triangles and one purple cloud shape for younger Heroes.
• Make sure Heroes write their names on their crafts.

Directions
Step 1: Spread glue on the front surface of the cardboard.

Step 2: Affix orange paper to glue. Wrap the paper edges over and around the edges of the cardboard. Secure the paper on the back of the cardboard with glue or tape. This is the base of your picture frame.

Step 3: Use the templates to trace 6 triangle shapes onto green paper, and a cloud on purple paper.

Tip: Placing the green triangles each at a bit of an angle will provide the hero starburst look.

Step 4: Help preschool Heroes to arrange the shapes on the frame and glue them down. Glue the triangles down first, then the cloud.

Step 5: Encourage them to decorate the frame with stickers, markers, and more.

Step 6: Have them to glue photos from their time at Hero Hotline in the middle of their frames!

Bible Tie-in
SAY: **At Hero Hotline, we've learned all about teaming up to serve God by bringing peace and lifting each other up. When you look at this frame with your pictures from Hero Hotline, remember that God's Heroes can do amazing things together!**

Bible Story
Unexpected Heroes Give Paul a Basket Ride
Acts 9:1-25

Hotline Verse
So let's strive for the things that bring peace and the things that build each other up.
(Romans 14:19)

Hotline Tip
Heroes are called to... Show Grace!

Materials
• **Hero Hotline Tablecloth** or other table covering
• **Hero Hotline Craft Theme Stickers**
• **Hero Hotline Stay-Put Glitter Stickers**
• Hero Team Frame Template (www.CokesburyVBS.com)
• cardboard for frame
• paper or card stock
• glue or glue sticks
• markers
• scissors
• tape
• ruler

Leader Tip
Re-use pizza, cereal, and other clean boxes for the cardboard.

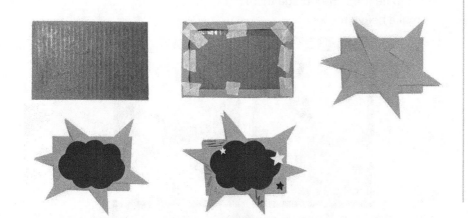

Make-It-and-Take-It Bible Craft
Light Resist Painting

Bible Story
Unexpected Heroes Give Paul a Basket Ride
Acts 9:1-25

Hotline Verse
So let's strive for the things that bring peace and the things that build each other up.
(Romans 14:19)

Hotline Tip
Heroes are called to... Show Grace!

Materials:
- **Hero Hotline Tablecloths**
- Light Artwork Hero Puppet coloring page (found in the Free Resources section at www.CokesburyVBS.com)
- flashlight
- plain white paper
- tape
- crayons
- yellow washable paint
- paintbrushes
- smocks

Purpose
Heroes will make a painting as a reminder of the Bible story.

Preparation
Cover the table with Hero Hotline Tablecloths or paper.

Directions

1. Have the children wear smocks.

2. Mount a piece of plain white paper on the wall. Show them the flashlight. Turn out the lights and shine the flashlight on the white paper.

3. Put your hand in front of the flashlight to create a shadow on the wall. Hold up two fingers to make a bunny. Give each child a turn making a shadow bunny.

SAY: **In our Bible story, Paul was blinded by a bright light.**

4. Give each child a piece of plain paper.

ASK: **How do you think Paul felt when he started out for the city to arrest followers of Jesus?**

SAY: **Paul might have been mad.**

5. Have the children use crayons to color their papers showing how it feels to be mad. Encourage them to make heavy marks.

SAY: **But something happened to change Paul. When Paul was traveling to a city named Damascus, he saw a bright light. The light was so bright he could not see.**

6. Show each child how to use the yellow paint to brush color over the crayon markings. The crayons will resist the paint. Set the paintings flat to dry.

SAY: **Paul heard the voice of Jesus. Then his friends led him into the city. A man named Ananias came and helped Paul see again. Ananias forgave Paul for wanting to hurt followers of Jesus. Ananias showed Paul grace. Heroes are called to show grace.**

SAY: **In our Bible story, some of Paul's friends helped him safely leave the city by hiding him in a basket. Paul's friends showed Paul grace. Heroes are called to show grace.**

Make-It-and-Take-It Bible Craft
Basket Rubbings

Purpose
Heroes will create a reminder of the Bible story and the Bible verse.

Preparation
Use a permanent marker to print the Bible verse on a piece of copy paper. Copy the verse for each child. Remove the papers from crayons. Set the woven items on the table.

Directions

1. Give each child the Bible verse paper and a crayon with the paper removed. Say the Bible verse with the children.

2. Help each child tape a piece of paper over the bottom of a basket, or on top of a woven place mat or plate.

3. Show the child how to rub over the paper with the side of the crayon. The texture of the basket will show through the paper. Encourage the children to try rubbing on different baskets to see the different textures.

SAY: **In our Bible story, some of Paul's friends helped him safely leave the city by hiding him in a basket. Paul's friends showed Paul grace. Heroes are called to show grace.**

Bible Story
Unexpected Heroes Give Paul a Basket Ride
Acts 9:1-25

Hotline Verse
So let's strive for the things that bring peace and the things that build each other up.
(Romans 14:19)

Hotline Tip
Heroes are called to... Show Grace!

Materials
- Hero Hotline Tablecloths or other table covering
- copy paper
- permanent marker
- different kinds of woven baskets, place mats, or plates
- paper
- crayons with the papers removed
- tape

Bible Story

Unexpected Heroes Give
Paul a Basket Ride
Acts 9:1-25

Hotline Verse

So let's strive for the
things that bring peace
and the things that build
each other up.
(Romans 14:19)

Hotline Tip

Heroes are called to...
Show Grace!

Materials:

• flashlights

Preschool Science
Flashlight Play

Preparation:

Make sure the flashlights have batteries.

Directions:

1. Show the children how to turn on
   the flashlights. Let them take turns
   shining the flashlights on the wall,
   on the table, or on the floor.

SAY: **A bright light helped a man
named Paul change from a person
who did not like Jesus to a person
who loved and followed Jesus.**

2. Play a game with the light. Shine
   the flashlight all over the floor and
   let the children chase the light.

What's Happening?

Open the flashlight and show the
batteries. When the flashlight is
turned on, the energy in the batteries
make the flashlight have a bright
light.

Preschool Science
Weight Lifting

Preparation:
Place the laundry basket in the center of the room.

Directions:

1. Have the children stand around the laundry basket.

2. Show them the items you have provided. Have them separate the items into light and heavy.

3. Choose a child to place a light item in the basket and lift it up.

ASK: **Is it hard to lift the basket?**

4. Give each child a turn placing a light item in the basket and lifting it up.

5. Let each child place a heavy item in the basket and lift it up.

ASK: **Is it harder to lift the basket now?**

6. Let the children discover which items make the basket easier or harder to lift.

7. Stand in the basket. Let one or two children try to lift you up. (Don't actually allow them to lift you.)

SAY: **Paul's friends helped Paul stay safe. Some of Paul's friends hid Paul inside a basket and then lowered him down the city wall inside the basket.**

ASK: **Do you think Paul's basket was heavy or light?**

SAY: **When Paul's friends helped Paul, they showed Paul grace. Heroes are called to show grace.**

ASK: **What are some ways we can show grace?** (*forgive someone, show love, be kind, be a good listener, pray for someone, help others*)

What's Happening?
Lighter objects are easier to lift; heavy items are harder to lift.

Bible Story
Unexpected Heroes Give Paul a Basket Ride
Acts 9:1-25

Hotline Verse
So let's strive for the things that bring peace and the things that build each other up.
(Romans 14:19)

Hotline Tip
Heroes are called to...
Show Grace!

Materials:
- laundry basket
- light objects to put in the basket: such as paper, feathers, and cotton balls
- heavy objects to put in the basket: such as blocks, books, and dolls

Bible Story
Unexpected Heroes Give Paul a Basket Ride
Acts 9:1-25

Hotline Verse
So let's strive for the things that bring peace and the things that build each other up.
(Romans 14:19)

Hotline Tip
Heroes are called to...
Show Grace!

Ingredients
• pre-packaged snacks
• scoop-style corn chips
• bear-shaped crackers or cookies

Supplies
• table
• basket
• string or yarn
• paper plates
• bowls
• table

Snacks

Down the Wall Snacks

Preparation
Turn a table over on the side. Place the treats inside a basket. Tie a length of yarn to the basket.

Directions
Have the children sit on the floor in front of the table.

SAY: **In our Bible story, Paul's friends help Paul stay safe by lowering him down the wall in a basket. Let's pretend our table is a city wall.**

1. Go behind the table and crouch down.

2. Use the yarn to lower the basket over the wall to the floor. Let the children choose a snack from the basket.

3. Say a thank-you prayer.

Scoop Up Paul

Preparation
Place gummy bears in bowls or shallow containers.

Directions
1. Give each child a paper plate. Place several corn chips on the plate.

2. Give each child a small bowl or cup with a few bear crackers.

3. Show the child how to use the corn chip to scoop up a bear from the bowl or a cup."

SAY: **Paul's friends helped Paul stay safe by lowering him down the wall in a basket. Let's pretend our scoops are the basket and the bear crackers are Paul.**

4. Have fun scooping up the bears and eating the snack.

5. Say a thank-you prayer.

Printed in the USA
CPSIA information can be obtained
at www.ICGtesting.com
LVHW010706091123
762955LV00001B/2

9 781791 024390